# OPEN BAR

My Journey in Opening a Billiard Room and Sports Bar

## DANNY KUYKENDALL, PhD

Open Bar

My Journey in Opening a Billiard Room and Sports Bar

Danny Kuykendall, PhD

Print ISBN: 978-1-54392-939-3

eBook ISBN: 978-1-54392-940-9

## Editor's note for Open Bar

This is a nonfiction book offering readers first hand knowledge about the ins and outs of opening a sports bar/poolroom/restaurant. The author is a successful owner of a billiards room and sports bar/restaurant, who shares his account of how he built the establishment over the course of 25 plus years.

The book is filled with lively and engaging stories that pop off the page, making this book an enjoyable read, even for those who have no interest in opening a restaurant. There is much wisdom and entertainment found in these pages, and readers of all kinds will be rewarded for spending time with the book. It is a personal account of following a vision, highlighting a personal philosophy and tracing the journey that led him through the stages; from dream, to planning, to opening, through hardships, lessons learned, and ultimate success.

The editor applied consistency of treatments throughout so that the reader can focus on the content of the book and not be distracted by a mischievous comma here and there.

It is hoped that any changes made by the editor do not alter the author's unique voice style, or intentions for the book. The author's voice is strong throughout and is engaging. Any changes made were to highlight this voice.

Bookbaby Publishing

# INTRODUCTION

I began working on Danny K's Billiards and Sports Bar 25 years ago, drawing up a sketch on graph paper of where the pool tables would be placed, the kitchen, bar, restrooms, etc. The old Powerhouse Gym had been vacant for over a year, and I had been eying this location for even longer, believing it to be an ideal location for my dream bar and restaurant. As I got closer to finalizing the paperwork that would make this space mine, the anticipation of finally opening the business of my dreams was palpitating. I had hoped for this through most of my adult life, and I couldn't believe my idea might finally come to fruition.

My passion for opening a billiard room began when I was just 19 years old. I recently contacted an old friend who told me that I had talked to him about my fantasy pool room when we were spending a weekend stint in a small jailhouse in southern Arizona. Any time I did something wrong in those days, I was thrown in jail. Maybe five times I saw the inside of a jailhouse, and it seemed that if I jaywalked or looked cross-eyed at a cop I ended up in the clink.

This was the late '60s, and the West Coast drug craze had rolled through Sierra Vista, Arizona, carrying almost the entire teenage population with it. I resisted at first, but found myself ostracized by close friends and relatives, and so I dove into the drug culture like everyone else. I became a businessman of sorts, running small amounts of marijuana from across the border in Agua Prieta, México, to Douglas, and then to Sierra Vista, portioning it into baggies, and selling it to the local population of GIs and other users.

After one unpleasantly long weekend in jail, I abandoned that line of business and took one of many regular jobs I would work in the next few years.

My parents divorced in 1969, my mother finally realizing that my father couldn't and wouldn't change his ways. So, at the age of 19, I moved to Phoenix with my father, while my mother remarried and moved to Orange County, California, with her new husband. Phoenix was a hotbed of all kinds of drugs, and I was trying to keep up with my peers in consuming as much as was humanly possible. I did not fit in well with this crowd, and was usually very uncomfortable around most of them. The drugs I experimented with didn't help much with my social skills either. LSD and I did not get along well. I still dropped it, even though every trip was a bummer. Why? I could not say no to my friends. I didn't want to appear mentally or emotionally weak, so I kept putting myself through this tortuous form of entertainment, each time hoping LSD would be kind to me, and each time experiencing nothing but another long, terrifying nightmare.

During this time, a girl I knew wanted to smuggle some Dexedrine (Dextroamphetamine) in from Mexico, and she had a foolproof plan. Dexedrine was mostly used as a diet pill in the late '60s, but strong doses worked as an upper and made the user feel euphoric for several hours. The plan was to travel to Nogales, Mexico, from Phoenix and buy Dexedrine capsules at a pharmacy across the border. The Dexedrine across the border was much stronger and would make for a much better high. After the purchase, she would sit in the back of my car and sew the pills into her tampon.

And so she sat in the backseat of the car, sewing those pills into a Kotex. Of course we had been observed by the US Border Patrol in Nogales the whole time, and eventually the red lights started flashing. We were pulled over in Patagonia, a few miles north of Nogales.

Was I scared! The agent said he saw us buy the drugs and knew we had them somewhere. I denied, denied, and denied some more. They brought in a local female officer to frisk the girl. She saw the tampon and did not investigate. We were scot-free and relieved—but it scared me enough to get off all drugs, including marijuana. I was losing my mind, and the fear of spending a few months in jail put me over the top. Some experiences in life are wake-up calls. This was a major one for me.

The drug chapter in my life, albeit traumatizing, taught me the importance of moderation and how to treat people. I was in a bad mental state for a few years, but these experiences helped shape the person I finally became. I have always had compassion for people, especially those who can do nothing about their situation. Most people at Danny K's will say that I care about others and genuinely try to understand where they're coming from. Even though they may not be experiencing as much difficulty as I was at the time, I still understand what they are going through. I am thankful for these experiences in my teenage years and that I was able to emerge from the problems of that time. I would not be as successful without them.

From this point on, I still hung around with all my friends, but I was the only person not taking drugs of any kind. It made me—and everyone else—very uncomfortable. I needed new friends and a new climate, so when my mother moved out to Anaheim with her new husband in 1970, I decided to live with them. I was in serious psychological turmoil, having removed myself from reality with a combination of drugs and neurosis, and I needed help desperately. My stepfather had noticed a mental health clinic on his way to work, and made the suggestion that I seek some help there. Chuck, my stepdad, was a good guy and saw that I was in emotional distress, and wanted to see me get better. He introduced me to Dr. Pierce Ommanney, a local psychologist who had an office in Anaheim, and I slowly emerged back into reality. I cannot thank Pierce enough for his help. Without him, I would not be here today. Of course I had to work on myself a lot, but God sent me help and gratefully I accepted it.

I then enrolled in Cypress College in 1973, majoring in psychology; entered Cal State Long Beach in 1976, and finished a master's degree at Cal State Los Angeles in 1981. I completed my PhD in psych in 1988 from a small tutorial program in San Diego, and sat for the California State Exam twice in the early '90s, coming close but not passing either time. So what did I do with the PhD? Opened a poolroom! Makes sense, right? The psychology background, however, has been very helpful in operating this business.

I made my living during college doing an odd assortment of jobs: donut fryer, delivering newspapers, working at a 7-Eleven convenience store, selling shoes, and finally, selling pool tables and billiard supplies. I was already playing pool at close to a professional level, and on weekends I could supplement my income by playing for money in local bars and poolrooms. By this time, I had stopped hustling. I would ask the person to play for money, and then play my best game. Often, my opponent would quit after the first game.

My first experience with pool was a game called caroms—a Christmas present from my mom. It was a board game that had rings (caroms) and four net pockets with a couple of pool cues. My brothers and I wouldn't use the cues, but just flicked the caroms with our middle finger. It was fun, but after playing on a regulation pool table, we were hooked on the real game of pool. Through the early years, my passion for pool never abated. I began as a 12-year-old, fashioning a pool table out of the dining room table by laying a blanket on top, using my father's golf balls and the handle of his putter as a makeshift pool cue. The golf balls would just drop onto the floor. I didn't care.

The YMCA in Bisbee, Arizona, was a decent place to shoot pool, and I spent as much time as possible knocking balls around. The dynamic of colliding spheres and the challenge of figuring out how to control them on a flat rectangular surface with pockets had me mesmerized. In 1963, our family moved to Douglas, Arizona, and I was able to play on a Brunswick 4 1/2 by 9 foot, ball return pool table recently installed in the local bowling alley. Coronado Lanes was directly on the way home from school, and I was attracted to that pool table like a magnet to iron. We would play for quarters or dimes . . . whatever would make the game interesting. Back then, pool table time cost a dollar an hour, no matter how many players, and sometimes we would play simply for the time. So I could play for cheap and make some money as well.

Much to my mother's chagrin, I continued to find a way to spend every free moment with a pool cue in my hand, attempting to slide these colliding spheres into one of six pockets. I was an average student, and my father's penchant for alcohol gave all the kids an excuse to avoid the books and do as we damn well pleased. My two brothers and I opted for pool. All of us loved the game. I was the one who made more time to play, and as time went on, I kept playing.

The Hustler, a movie starring Paul Newman about small-time pool hustler "Fast Eddie" Felson, had debuted in 1961, and pool was extremely popular for about 10 years afterward. Poolrooms sprang up everywhere in the early '60s, and luckily for us, Coronado Lanes had these great, brand-new, Brunswick Gold Crown pool tables. Brunswick was franchising modern poolrooms, reflecting the decor of the '60s. The rooms were clean, well kept, and decent. Heaven! A lot of kids in high school would stop by after school and play, and I was quickly becoming the school pool shark. Not exactly what my parents wanted me known for. I was thrilled to pick up a few bucks, though, and earn some spending money by doing something I would have done happily for free. It was nice to see pool gravitate away from the smoke-filled rooms that hustlers and schemers frequented.

Also in Douglas there was a bar and poolroom named the B & P Tavern, built sometime in the early 1900s. The place had spittoons on oak floors and perpetually smelled like stale beer and cigar smoke. The ball return tables were made near the turn of the century and had a way of taking us back in time. This room was really a throwback to pre-Depression poolrooms where only men attended. Very seldom would any woman go in the place. (My brother Jim recently made the comment, "Estrogen could not have lasted for more than about 10 seconds in there.") Honestly, I miss the atmosphere, and don't believe that there are any remaining poolrooms like it in the nation. But it's okay; make way for progress . . .

The house rules in this old poolroom called for anyone under 18 to be accompanied by an adult. So we would give a bum who was sitting in the back corner a quarter, and he would be our chaperone for the day. The poolroom owner didn't mind. He made money off us shooting pool, so everyone was happy. It cost 10 cents for a rack, and the rack boy's name was Pete. He was there to rack the balls when a game was finished. We would buy a coke if we had a dime, and play for the cost of the rack. There was a lot of history in that room; it unfortunately closed down 25 years ago or so.

When we moved to Sierra Vista, Arizona, in 1967, my brothers and I immediately scoped out the local poolrooms. Home to a dozen Gold Crown pool tables, the Playland Arcade was situated next door to the Fort Huachuca Army base. I continued my obsession for pool and found that I could hustle a few bucks from the Army guys coming over to the city to blow their monthly ration of cash. They were in AIT camp, which followed boot camp and was the step just before deployment to Vietnam. Looking back, I regret hustling any of these guys for their extra money; it was a hard time for this country and a distressing time for GIs who were forced to fight in such an unpopular war. When I look back on that kid I once was, I see a family on the verge of falling apart, a father who couldn't stay off the booze, and kids who were finding avenues to express our discontent with his addiction. I suppose hustling was how I expressed mine.

I had many memorable experiences with these GIs who were stationed in Sierra Vista for a couple of months before being shipped off to Vietnam. I played an Army guy once at the local bowling alley, and won 10 games in a row of eight ball for $5 a game. I would have to say that I threw off some, and didn't reveal my true skill. The second he quit, four or five of his friends came in and one said, "We're just gonna have to take your damned money back!" And they weren't looking to play me for it.

I was, of course, shaking in my boots. But the young man who lost said quietly, "I lost fair and square—let's just leave."

And so after another couple of close encounters, and the fact that I was genuinely beginning to feel bad about hustling these guys, I decided I would play my best game, no matter the outcome. My best friend in college, Ron Foss, complained about this, because he knew we could make more money if I held back and didn't play my best game at first. I apologized but let him know that there was no alternative for me. I needed to live with myself after I won money.

One time in the '70s I encountered a high roller who had just come from Los Alamitos Race Track with a load of cash, and he wanted to play. We were at a local bar in Anaheim that had a few pool tables. So we played for $20 a game of eight ball, and I won 7 games in a row. He good-naturedly chuckled and said that I could have at least let him win a game, and he could have lost quite a bit more money if I had played him right.

My buddy Ron was not laughing.

Sorry, not the way I operated.

I usually played for $5 or $10 a game, and mostly eight ball, because most bar players were familiar with this game. In 1976, at a place in Anaheim called the Corner Pocket (which is still there, I believe), I played a big biker by the name of Dirty John. He was a little intimidating by his size alone, and obviously he was a tough, street-wise motorcycle guy. I'm not sure how he got his nickname, and I really didn't want to know. We were playing for five and then 10, and I was ahead about 70 bucks, and he asked to play one game for 50. I normally would not have played for 50, but his friend had just arrived with a big Bowie knife on his side, and in that atmosphere I decided to be agreeable and not make waves. So we played one game for 50. John was a pretty good player, and so I made sure I ran the table after I broke and made a ball. I motioned to a pocket to make the eight ball in (when playing eight ball, a pocket needs to be called), but I did not verbally call the pocket. Dirty John looked at me and said, "Sorry, man, you didn't call the pocket."

Well, I could see I was horribly outnumbered and at an extreme disadvantage, so like a person confronting a ferocious animal I sat at the bar and said, "Goddammit, I called the eight ball, and I'm going to sit here until I get my fucking money!" I was going to show no fear, even though underneath my facade I was petrified.

John looked at me sideways, probably thinking I was some sort of fool for standing up to him and his crowd. But he respected that I had the guts to stand up to him, and suggested we play another game. I assented to that, ran the table again, and made sure I verbally called the eight ball. I won. He said, "Okay, now we're even." I could live with that. I bought him and his friends a beer, and managed to sneak out alive with my winnings. Later I saw John somewhere else and he said, "The way you stood up to me I thought you knew Kung Fu or something." (Kung Fu was really popular back then . . . you know, David Carradine). He didn't realize how truly scared I was.

All the years I played pool in bars, I never once had to fight anyone. A professional pool player once told me, "Don't ever fight over a pool game. The guy you're playing usually can't beat you anyway, so what are you risking? Why get yourself hurt?" I have always been able to talk myself out of trouble (knock on wood). I became one of the better players in Southern California back in the late 1970s.

At left Dan Kuyken-dall sizes up his next shot before he goes on to place second in men's billiards.

*Yours truly playing in a collegiate tournament in Berkeley. I was 26. Came in 2nd place.*

I want to mention some who influenced me, and mentors who helped me along in the sport. Wayne Norcross helped me with the game of straight pool and encouraged me to play in all the tournaments that I could afford. Buddy Hall with his great stroke and unmatched nine ball game was also supportive and set a good example of how to play the game and not become upset, true sportsmanship. And, Efren Reyes, who did not directly teach me anything, but I learned so much just by watching the magician at work. He is probably the greatest all-round pool player of all time.

*In the mid 80's taking a break from a pool tournament in Reno. Finished 9-12 in the Reno Open.*

I was selling shoes for Nordstrom at the time, and had the opportunity to sell billiard supplies in early 1980 for Golden West Billiards in Orange. Since this retail business was very small, it gave me the opportunity to delve into the mechanisms that make a small business tick, such as cost of goods, net profit, and marketing. Marketing is probably the most important of these skills. Though all the basics of business are necessary, successful marketing can make or break a business. Working for Golden West, I was able to read and study a profit and loss statement, and get a feel for what it really costs to run a small business.

Of all my random job experiences, working for Nordstrom's Department Store as a women's shoe seller was the most valuable.

Their slogan, "The only difference between us and other department stores is the way we treat our customers," is something that every small business owner should heed carefully. I carried this notion into the billiards industry and found that I was creating repeat business through courtesy and genuine care for customers. This focus is what I consider to be the crux of internal marketing.

*In the late 80's I began my own wholesale cue company. I would carry over 300 pool cues.*

I eventually became burnt out on managing and selling pool tables and supplies. I did it for about 10 years, and dealing with the public in a sales capacity took its toll on me. I began searching for a different way to make a living while I studied for the California State Psychological Exam, and found it selling wholesale billiard cues with a partner. We would travel to Reno, Phoenix, even as far as Texas to sell our products. After about six months, we split the business up and went our own ways. Let's just say we had irreconcilable differences. This turned out to be a good thing, because I could work out of my van at my own pace. After about a year or so I had most of the customers anyway, because I was knowledgeable, dependable, and gave everyone a little credit. So, for about four years I owned and operated DK Cues, and traveled around the Southwest selling cues and supplies to the numerous poolrooms that had opened in the wake of 1986 Scorsese film The Color of Money, with Paul Newman reprising his role as "Fast Eddie" Felson.

*Me shooting pool in the early 90's.*

During these years of shooting pool, working, and going to school, I was searching for a billiard room location to call my own. My idea from the very beginning was to have an upper-class room serving excellent food from a full kitchen, and an assortment of draft beers and mixed drinks. The pool tables would be first class and kept in top condition at all times. And the venue would also offer sports on TVs, even though in the early '90s sports bars were not as popular as they would become years later. The service would be only the best, and we would develop a regular clientele.

My billiard experience and expertise are only a fraction of what I use in my business as a whole. I could open a similar operation without having had any billiard experience. As long as the pool tables are maintained in good condition, then an ordinary billiard room can succeed. My passion for billiards may have been the impetus for opening a poolroom in the first place, but the business model I operate under has little to do with pool.

I opened Danny K's Café and Billiards in 1994, and after a few years of struggle made it into one of the most successful operations of its kind in the nation. And struggle is no exaggeration. Several months of working 16-hour days and barely being able to keep the doors open teaches the true meaning of the word struggle. After a few years, my partner and I finally made a decent salary and felt the glow of some success.

This book is a narrative of how I managed to create a business that I have a passion for, how I maintained a successful operation, and how I kept my love for life as well, without letting the work consume me. Restaurant owners typically are so enmeshed in their business they have trouble allowing the business to leave their thoughts when they're away, even when taking a vacation or playing a round of golf. A restaurant owner should be able to psychologically set aside his involvement in the business just as a day worker finishes his job and doesn't think about it again until he arrives at work the next day. How can we fulfill a lifelong dream as small business owners, make our businesses successful enough to meet our aspirations, and then allow it to run well when we are not around? This, I believe, is the ultimate objective of the small business owner: financial success while pursuing your vision, the ability to enjoy the fruits of your labor, and freedom from worry about the business when you are not physically there. My early experiences helped me grow into the person who opened Danny K's Billiards and Sports Bar in 1994. Over the course of the next 25 years, I had to learn how to manage my business and my life in ways that were mutually satisfying. My passion for billiards, the effect of the drugs and resulting trauma, the string of odd jobs and shooting pool on weekends to make ends meet, the degrees in psychology, managing the billiard supply, and then wholesale cue sales have all contributed to my ability to run a large establishment such as this. The experiences gave me the raw material from which I was able to make a dream come true business. The tests and lessons learned along the way positioned me to take the leap of faith, and to sustain that optimism by finding opportunity in setbacks. Although sometimes difficult, my life has been filled with events and experiences that have given me the patience and know-how to make the right decisions, sometimes under tremendous pressure.

# A PASSION FOR A DREAM

I've often witnessed entrepreneurs make a common mistake when opening a small business. They place their desire to make money over and above a passion or interest in their product or service. When we venture out on our own and invest all our savings, borrow all we are able, including mortgaging our homes and tapping out all credit cards, a deep passion and interest for the product or service should drive this endeavor. The aftermath of failure can be devastating.

Ten years ago, I spoke with a middle-aged man aspiring to open a nightclub in a popular area in north Orange County. He was seeking my counsel about the viability of this particular operation. The location he had in mind was the site of a once failed nightclub, but it was a good area and had the template for what he wanted; the kitchen only needed equipment, the dance floor was in the area he had planned for as well as the entrance and seating area. All that was needed was a remodel and facelift, the purchase of furniture, kitchen equipment, point of sale system, and so on.

After speaking with him for a while I realized that he had very little experience or interest in nightclubs. He and his wife had enjoyed ballroom dancing at one time, and that was his impetus for thrusting himself headfirst into the nightclub business. Of course, owning and operating a nightclub involves a great deal more than only promoting the dance aspect. He had no independent business experience up to this point, and had made a living working for the phone company most of his life. He had neither bar nor restaurant experience. The rent in this particular location was extremely high, and with other operating costs, the business would have to be immediately successful to cover all operating expenses. He noted that he could do most of the remodeling himself and that, "All I need to get motivated is for someone to tell me I can't do it."

I strongly advised this man against the endeavor. I noted the high lease payments, the hidden costs of running a small business such as liability insurance, worker's comp, unexpected repairs, added payroll for security in the evenings, among many other expenses. However, if he felt determined to pursue this idea, I recommended that he work as a bartender for a while and possibly as a part-time cook to learn the food trade. He dismissed all of these suggestions. Needless to say, within six months he was out of business and in the throes of bankruptcy.

Maybe his passion lay somewhere else other than a nightclub operation. An independent phone service perhaps? Or maybe he could have taken one of his hobbies and pursued a business in which he had a genuine interest and sincere passion and joy for, such as a ballroom dancing instructor. Meanwhile, the entirety of his family savings was lost, and the strain it placed on his family was horrific. We only hear of businesses going under, not the aftermath and negative effects the families endure.

To withstand the first few years of a mediocre business, making only a small profit, we at least need to have the passion necessary to endure the trials and tribulations of achieving our dream. The business operator needs to have the dedication to work 16-hour days on a small salary and risk personal relationships to achieve a goal that may take years to reach. It's common knowledge that 75 percent of restaurant-related businesses fail in the first three years, and 90 percent fail within five years. If a person enters into the business with a "pie in the sky" attitude, reality usually sets in after a couple of months when payroll and rent are difficult to pay. Then the work really begins. Hard choices have to be made, cutting expenses to the bone and laying off employees who aren't really needed. What is it worth for the business to survive?

My passion lay in the billiards industry, and especially in the area people enjoy the most: shooting pool. And what a better thing to enjoy shooting pool, than with an ice-cold beer and a great hamburger, steak, or salad? And how about a professional baseball game on a high-definition TV to top it all off? If I could offer all of these things, would the public come? I believed they would.

One mistake I made was opening with too little capital. All the money I used was borrowed at a moderate to high interest rate. Also, even though I had worked as a bar manager for a while and was proficient in parts of the industry, I lacked experience in managing an operation of this size, and had almost no kitchen background. I was expecting higher gross sales and a higher net profit than was realistic. Without a sincere passion for this dream, I might not have rolled up my sleeves and made the necessary changes to the business to insure its survival.

I had attributes to manifest my dream business over the long haul. I had scoped out different locations for 10 years, written numerous business proposals to lure investors and use as a template for operating procedures, and had gone through many rejections from city planning commissions and potential investors who didn't want to risk their hard-earned money on anything other than a sure deal.

I was so intent on opening a place that I would drive by a location several times, and imagine the poolroom of my dreams there. I'd call the leasing agent and ask for the rent being charged, and then find out after I called the city that the zoning was not the right one for a poolroom. I soon learned to call the city first and ask about the zoning for a poolroom opening in that location. That saved time and energy I had previously been putting into a dream room that was never a possibility.

After discovering a dozen or so locations that failed to open for one reason or another, did I ever consider abandoning my dream? Never. Sure, I was discouraged after some of the more promising ventures failed to open, but I maintained my passion until I could finally open a viable business. And, consider the business experience I achieved while working on these failed locations. My business proposals got better, I was able to deal with the particular city planning commission with more knowledge and persuasion, and I was more prepared to rise to the occasion and make the business a success when it finally opened. These failures were very important lessons, because I learned more with each endeavor; why a city will not allow you to open, or, how an investor may back out because the parking is insufficient. It's all about gaining knowledge, experience, and maturity for the time when it is really needed.

If an entrepreneur has an inner, sincere passion for the endeavor, he will also have a feel for what will fail and what will succeed. Usually one source or another will argue that this is not the right location, or parking is not adequate, rent is too high, a partner wants too great an interest in the business, etc. Paying attention to our intuition and apprehensions will usually deter us from forcing a business to open that will eventually fail. It's imperative to stay in touch with the dream on an emotional level, so inner intuition is used to recognize warning signals that arise in the process of trying to open.

Several years ago, I heard Ross Perot discuss his dream of offering an outside computer service for large corporations. Once he got started on his dream, he had no choice but to see it through to fruition. This is how I felt about opening Danny K's. Once I got started, I had no option but to complete the mission. The cliché "baptism by fire" is the most accurate description of experiencing the initial pitfalls of opening a restaurant and/or sports bar. I was told it would be difficult. I just could not imagine what I would eventually have to go through to stay alive in the business. I only thank God that I had the passion for my dream.

Several poolrooms opened in the wake of the release of *The Color of Money* in 1986. More than a dozen rooms had opened in the Inland Empire and Palm Springs alone by 1990, and maybe one of these places is still open today. Because the movie was so popular, businesses could open with a few pool tables and a small bar and actually do pretty well.

I remember a place in Palm Desert that was failing as a used furniture store, and the owner just added a few pool tables and a cooler for cokes and managed to stay in business for about a year! Most of these places were riding the wave of popularity that the movie created, and many of them were gone within a couple of years. I doubt that many of these entrepreneurs had any real passion for this type of business.

My experience in the retail billiard industry drove me to finally see my dream to fruition. I had become so tired of selling retail billiard supplies that I feared suffering a permanent negative personality change if I didn't do something different. And so I started selling pool cues wholesale to billiard rooms as a way to segue my way out of selling retail. I was dealing with retailers instead of the public, and that was a good change. This also enabled me to gain a fresh outlook and gave me time to work harder on my life's dream.

When we opened Danny K's in January of 1994, my partner and I were full of ambition and enthusiasm to make this venture a success. Danny K's opened strong and appeared to be on its way to becoming really profitable. However, we had a couple of issues hindering us in the beginning. We were underfunded, and were borrowing money at a high interest rate, well past opening.

And those loans and lines of credit had payments that were due immediately. Even though we were making a modest profit, that net profit was going toward paying off the borrowed money. Checks started bouncing six months after opening. We had only beer and wine for sale, no hard liquor. This put a ceiling on the amount of overall sales, because typically, one or more people in a group want to enjoy a mixed drink or a shot of alcohol. We started strong but began to slow down after a few months.

For these reasons, Danny K's was struggling to survive in the first two years of business. We did not know which check would bounce next, but figured they would not all go through. And of course it was the rent check that bounced. Then another rent check failed to go through. We were threatened with having to vacate the property. We were on the brink of going under, and it was a very scary time. But I took necessary steps to stem the bleeding. I let all three managers go, and cut all waste out of monthly spending. We had smoke eaters rented at $700 per month. Gone. All unnecessary expenses were cut out completely, or at least pared to a minimum. After a while, we began to break even. Checks stopped bouncing.

Meanwhile, the hard going in the beginning set us up for an excellent precedence for the future. I never became complacent about the business, and never took for granted any successes. Complacency, by the way, is the enemy of any small business. A capable CPA once told me, "There are usually two reasons that a business goes under.

The first is lack of funding. The second is complacency." Owners can feel that they have it made and slack off, allowing others to do everything for them. It is important to appreciate success and never become complacent. There but for the grace of God go all of us.

Is this endeavor what you really want to do with your life? Are you willing to devote 10 years or more to living and breathing a job that will eventually pay off, but initially will show very little profit? Is this part of your destiny in life? These are crucial questions to ask before risking it all on a life-changing occupation.

If you are considering opening a small business, I believe this book will enlighten you on just how committed you need to be before taking the step of signing a lease and venturing into the competition of making a business really successful. Even though it is a true commitment of time, money, effort, and this esoteric thing we call a soul, it is rewarding like very few things in life can be. After 25 years, I can truly say that it was worth the effort!

# A BAPTISM BY FIRE

I think it's important to explain the ordeals my partner and I experienced when opening Danny K's Billiards and Sports Bar. Opening a business of this size is not for the timid or faint of heart. Baptism by fire is an understatement.

We wanted to be the very best of any poolroom in the country, but found it increasingly difficult to raise money. In 1993 when we first looked at Danny K's location and knew this was the right place, we were filled with anticipation and excitement for the business we would generate and money we would make. One problem— the economy was going through a mild recession, and funds were difficult to come by.

My partner Richard mortgaged his home for a quarter of a million dollars, and was certain that he could come up with more money. I had some cash, and I had the ability to get some credit, but my main contribution was my expertise and general knowledge of how to build and operate a business such as this.

Money started running out even before we opened. Since we wanted first-class everything, we decided to spare no expense on building out the area, which had been a Gold's Gym and then a Powerhouse Gym before closing down in 1992. Though we used existing restrooms, plumbing, etc., we added a four-piece crown molding that ran the entire perimeter of Danny K's. It took a full five weeks to complete the crown molding alone, and the expenses just kept building. (The crown molding still looks great, so it was worth it in the end, I think.)

Then the plumber realized that the plumbing we had installed was not to code, and the pipes all needed to be replaced. Also, I had okayed slate for the restroom floors. Big mistake. The health department requires a light, neutral color for the kitchen and restroom floors. The slate had to be jack-hammered out and replaced by a typical kitchen floor tile. All this took extra time and money. We had to open soon, because we were already in the hole.

*The flooring looked great, but I soon found out that the health department wanted a light-colored floor! My bad.*

Richard's wife was nice enough to loan us money, but this was still not enough. My mother had done well in business in prior years, and she loaned us another $50,000. We were still way short. My partner had a friend who loaned us $60,000 at a high interest rate. Still we struggled with cash.

Finally, we opened in January of 1994, with no money in the bank and owing about a half million dollars. No one knew the stress that Richard and I were under. We had to make money right away, because we had to pay back borrowed money, and keep the business afloat. Richard's mortgage was one payment, his wife another, the friend who had loaned money needed to be paid, as well as leases

I signed. My mother was willing to wait on her money because she didn't need it right away. She was the only one who could wait, though.

We opened with only beer and wine, because the owners of the building at the time did not want hard alcohol sold on their premises. They thought it would attract a rough crowd. The problem with only having beer and wine is that many customers like a mixed drink or having a shot of some kind. And if a crowd of people are going out, they usually choose a place that can satisfy everyone's thirst.

And so, even though we opened with a flourish, business slowed down due to our lack of hard alcohol. There were other factors as well, but this was the most prominent. I spoke with a liquor distributor from Southern Wine and Spirits, and asked him how selling liquor would affect gross sales. He said about 20 percent. That may not seem like a lot, but he turned out to be close to accurate, and with the pour cost on alcohol being lower, it made a big difference.

I got married four months after Danny K's opened, and so now I had a wife to support (she was working—thank God) on top of teetering on the edge of going out of business. My partner and I would write ourselves a small paycheck, so we could meet our own personal expenses, only to have those checks bounce. And if those checks didn't bounce, then one here or there sent to a purveyor would not clear. The wolves were at the door, and the snouts were poking through.

While standing at the bar one day making a delivery, the Budweiser driver looked me in the eye and said, "What are you going to do when this place takes a dump?" He may as well have stuck me in the side with a harpoon. We were so close to going under that deliveries would soon be demanding cash, and we had no cash. Then came the icing on the cake: our rent check had not gone through, and a county marshal came to the bar, and yelled so everyone could hear, "Pay rent or quit." This was an order from the landlord. I was not at the business when this happened, but the bartender called me. We were in dire straits.

My mother came out from Texas on another visit, and looked at our profit and loss statement. She told us that we were making a profit, but we owed so much in opening costs that the money was all going out to creditors. She said we needed to stop spending money, and ASAP. So I told my partner Richard to not spend a dime unless I knew what the expense was, and I cut Danny K's spending to the bone. We began to eke out a profit. I also let go of all three managers that we had opened with, and all the servers and kitchen help who were not absolutely necessary. Slowly we began to pull out of the fire.

We also did not pay a few purveyors right away. We owed $10,000 to a food distributor whom I was sure had made a deal with my original general manager, maybe giving him a percentage. Our food cost was 58 percent! Way above any average for a restaurant or a sports bar. A friend of mine in the industry told me, "Don't pay them right now," and so I didn't, and it bought us a few months to heal. We slowly paid Rycoff Foods for the bill, but it took a few months.

*My mother Vivian was a help in the beginning, with General Manager Jami Jun. Jami began working here three weeks after we opened.*

The value of this baptism by fire was that I had to learn every job that existed at Danny K's. At times, I would fill in for a cook, or if a bartender could not make it, I would fill in. And I needed to learn the entire POS system. I was computer illiterate and resistant, but I sat down and stuck with it. Learning this way is the best way, though it's not easy. It sticks with you, because it is of the utmost importance to get it right.

I was told by the electrician, Tony, that we did not have enough amperage on our panel to handle all of the electrical input at Danny K's. But we couldn't afford another panel. We had a total of 200 amps and we needed at least 400, he said. In the first summer, there were times when half of the building would just go dark.

Talk about pressure! I would spend hours upstairs trying to figure out the problem, only to walk down and face all the customers at the bar pouring sweat and a look of pure exasperation on my face. But, the show must go on. We eventually afforded another 200 amps. In the meantime, I had to turn off some circuits so the panel would not shut down. This underscored the pressure I experienced in the first few years.

Danny K's was just over 10,000 square feet. We opened with what air conditioning was already there. We opened in January, so we figured we would be able to afford more A/C by the summer. We figured wrong. We couldn't afford anything like another air conditioning unit. When summer rolled around, it was extremely hot inside the building. There was an old existing A/C unit on the east side of the building and an antiquated unit on the west side. Not nearly enough to cool 10,000 square feet in the middle of summer. So customers came in and suffered, unless they were directly underneath the A/C unit.

"Danny, why is it so hot in here?"

I didn't know what to say. "This is your opportunity to lose weight!" They knew I couldn't afford the expense of a new unit. I would crack a joke, but it still stung that I could not accommodate my customers and make them comfortable. Within a year or two, we were able to install an A/C unit in the middle of Danny K's and add on our 200-amp electrical panel. It was still uncomfortably hot at times, but much better.

My schedule was almost around the clock. I would open Danny K's at 7 a.m., work past noon till about 2 p.m., go home and take a nap, come back to work, and close the business down at 1 or 2 a.m. One afternoon after we had been open for about six months, I decided to take the afternoon off and spend it with my wife, Claudia. We were relaxing, watching TV, when I received a phone call from the person at the front desk. It went something like, "Danny, a fight has broken out, and one of the pool tables is covered in blood. The police are here now."

Okay, great—the first chance I had for a day off, and I needed to go and take care of a crime that occurred at my business. The police being called is never a good thing, because the business can get a bad reputation with the police department, and then they are always watching you. I drove down to Danny K's, and saw a policeman speaking to a man outside who had his shirt off, and was bleeding some. I went inside to get the story from the bartender.

Apparently, a man who was drunk came and sat at the bar and began insulting the bartender. He was obviously very inebriated and looking for a fight. My day bartender Bubba was still there as well, sitting at the bar and watching what was happening. He spoke to the man and asked, "Is it necessary to insult the bartender?" This was all it took for the drunk to begin throwing fists. Bubba tried walking to the front desk to call the police. The man caught up with him and tried to grab him. Bubba, an ex–Navy Seal, immediately got him in a headlock, pulled him on top of a pool table, and started slugging him in the face. The cloth of the pool table was soaked in blood. When the police came, the man tried to fault us for the entire ordeal, claiming we had "provoked him" and "caused him to lash out."

I told the policeman what both bartenders had told me, and the cop just said, "Well, this man disagrees and wants to file a complaint."

I was thinking, Well, this is all I need—on top of being underwater financially, almost going fully under, now a lawsuit.

I looked toward the front door, and here comes the drunk, shirt off and dancing around like an idiot, ready to fight again. And so, I tell the cop, "There's your man who wants to file a complaint!"

The cop dealt with the man, came back to me, and said, "He's willing to let it go if you will."

Needless to say, no one filed a lawsuit and the incident became just another unusual experience at a bar. I can say now, after being open for 25 years, that we very seldom have had incidents of this kind. But back then the place was forming its identity, and once in a while something like this would happen. Now customers and the community understand that we have an unwritten code of conduct. You just don't do that kind of thing at Danny K's.

Another incident that occurred near the same time as this fight was another learning experience for me. I was hosting a Southern California pool tournament, and there were 64 players, mostly pros, participating. This was 1994, and pool was still relatively popular after The Color of Money had debuted in the late 1980s. We managed to add a little money to the event in order to get a full field of players, and we hosted the players and onlookers in the main room at Danny K's.

There was a professional player, whom I won't name here—let's call him Billy. Billy was a very good player and maybe a lower rated pro, but he was eccentric, and as time passed it seemed he might be becoming paranoid and possibly schizophrenic. He would order a twist-off-cap beer, and tell the bartender that he wanted to open it himself, because he thought someone wanted to poison him. He was playing that day of the tournament, and our lady house pro came up to me and said, "Danny, Billy is really going nuts. You've got to get him out of here."

I acted as I always did and still do. I was forthright and calm, and told Billy he had to go.

He resisted, but our bartender Bubba came over and said, "Billy, come with me. You have to leave."

He left, and I thought, problem solved.

I think I was playing in a match, and as I looked towards the entrance, I saw these decorative dry reeds that were in vases had been set on fire. Flames were gushing to the ceiling, and I was the first person in the room to notice.

I yelled out in a falsetto voice, "Fire!" Not sure why my voice was screechy, but I guess I was scared. I began running through pool tables, players, and spectators so I could somehow put out this fire. I could see that it was reaching the ceiling and it could escalate into a major situation if something was not done right away.

Fortunately, I have some loyal customers who are also just good people. Ken, a regular, whom I had known for a few years before opening my business, came running, turned over the vase the reeds were in, and rolled it outside. He suffered a couple of minor burns, but he was okay. Just another strange incident at Danny K's. And another lesson for me.

Outside, I looked around after helping put out the flames, and there was Billy, looking at me. I said, "Really, Bill?" He just looked at me and said nothing. We called the police, and they did what they could, but no one saw him light the plants on fire, and he was let go.

This and many other similar incidents made me who I became several years down the road—a person who does not overreact to emergencies or situations that might create panic in others. I believe that a quiet mind is always a good thing, even in the most turbulent situations.

Several years later Danny K's was broken into and robbed of $15,000. That was not easy, but everyone around me could see that I was not going to lash out emotionally over it. We were able to retrieve most of our stolen property through insurance, and we upgraded the doors and bought a heavier safe. Lesson learned, adjustments made, life goes on. It never pays to lose control of your emotions; it is easier to fix the problem in the right way while remaining calm.

One thing I want to underscore is the importance of being frugal with business expenses. Unfortunately, we needed to cut spending dramatically to save the business. Once I began cutting expenses to the bone, we were able to pay all the necessary invoices. It should be a policy to never waste money on anything for the business. Everything purchased should be a necessary expense, or something you know will enhance the atmosphere of the business and eventually add more income.

*My food distributor and good friend Steve Chiaramonte helped
me out with good advice in a financial crisis.*

When there's room in the budget, we are always upgrading TVs and carpet, repainting, adding seating, or remodeling the bar. The customers appreciate money being put back into the business, even if they don't consciously notice it. My ex-wife had difficulty with money being spent on the business. She couldn't see why I didn't just take all the profit out and put it in our bank account. This is one reason I am single now. (Of course, not the only reason.) Since my divorce, I'm spending more money to improve the business, and I'm making more money in profits. Spending money wisely creates good will, and customers notice and reward you for the care you essentially are giving to them through enhancing their experience.

The first few years of a business such as Danny K's is likely to be fraught with unexpected difficulties, major and minor. I suggest making a conscious effort to remember that this trying time will yield an end result that is fulfilling emotionally and financially if you give it your all. The Baptism by Fire is something that most business owners will go through in the beginning or in the first few years of business, no matter how prepared they are for the particular business they are in. Handling difficulties with calm and staying the course in the eye of the storm is essential for keeping stress to a minimum and ultimately for protecting your own mental health. Eventually, the lessons will be learned. The business will become established, and the end will be well worth the effort.

# GAINING EXPERIENCE

Any new business endeavor requires a considerable amount of practical, hands-on experience. An entrepreneur beginning his first business venture is remiss if he doesn't work in the field of his interest and passion. Sometimes on-the-job training can be overwhelming when initially entering a highly competitive market, whatever the type of business they plan to open. Are you prepared and experienced enough to risk everything you own to manage a competitive operation in which many other businesses are wooing the same customers?

If a billiard room that serves microwave sandwiches and bottled beer is what you want, I would recommend finding a job working behind the desk of a successful operation that fits this mold. How are the pool tables timed? Are the pool tournaments successful? If they are, how much food and beverage are consumed by the players? Why do customers continue to return and spend their hard-earned money? Are the evenings filled with casual players enjoying a beverage and a game of pool?

Ask the owner of any room you might like to emulate (if he's willing to divulge the information) about gross sales and net profit. Does the net profit figure provide you with a substantial income and lifestyle? You might try working the front desk in a pool room. It will also give you a feel for handling money and making change.

A sports bar or even a small bar is usually an attractive and highly-sought-after business by those entering business ownership for the first time. You can gain good, practical experience by working as a bartender or even a waiter in a larger operation, and you can see firsthand if this is really what you want to do. Sports bars usually have complete kitchens, as does Danny K's, and volunteering to work a few shifts in a kitchen can give you a valuable view of preparing food the right way and of conserving food cost. Some months or even years spent learning this way may be worth every minute invested if it propels your business success, or helps you avoid a costly mistake. As stated by the great King Leonidas of the Spartan empire, "The more troops sweat in training, the less they will bleed in combat." And believe me, not being able to make monthly rent is tantamount to dying on the battlefield—only it's a slower, more painful death.

A combination sports bar/billiard room/restaurant is a bit more complex than a billiard room or sports bar, and requires more owner involvement. If this more complex establishment is the type of operation you would like to pursue, then dabbling in all of these categories is a valuable weapon to have in your arsenal. Tackling a larger operation requires experience in at least two of these entities, and having knowledge of all three is preferred.

My business knowledge and background was very helpful in making Danny K's a success. Since operating a sports bar/billiard room is essentially a small business with similar categories of expenses to any type of operation, any experience in small business is useful. Even if the business is out of your home and a complement to your existing income, the experience of running a business will eventually come in handy.

My background was largely in billiards—retail, wholesale, and the playing end of the game. I had also worked as a manager at a beer bar for a few months to learn the bar trade. I had been a shoe salesman for a few years in my late twenties—a profession that gave me a foundation for customer service. I worked for Nordstrom department store from 1979 to 1980 selling ladies' shoes, and this is where I was taught the true meaning of customer service, an essential quality for any successful business.

Since I was regularly playing in pool tournaments in different billiard rooms, I studied layouts of pool tables, and where the front desk, restrooms, bar, and kitchen were located—and as a customer I could analyze what worked and what didn't. I also recorded to memory certain aspects of billiard rooms that were unique and which I personally liked, so I could incorporate these details into the design of my own room. The raised area at Danny K's was copied from Hard Times Billiards in Bellflower. Never be afraid to use someone else's idea. Everyone copies everyone else. Some poolrooms use similar furniture to mine, and I've noticed that the walls and ceilings are the same color as mine. I don't mind. Imitation is the sincerest form of flattery.

I had also worked in retail, and in 1980 I became manager of Golden West Billiards in Orange, in charge of service crews and retailing new and used pool tables and billiard accessories. Right away, I was able to study the process of operating a small business in the real world (not in a textbook): the importance of keeping labor costs down, of selling product at a decent profit. The concept of overall cost versus gross sales is essential to any small business. This experience also taught me the endless amount of expenses involved in running a small business. I was able to view the company profit-loss sheet that detailed all the seemingly endless expenses. I could see clearly why a small business is not always a cash cow.

Although it is important to have a positive attitude about your new business, it is also important to realize the nickels and dimes that tally the expenses involved, and how difficult it can be to earn a decent net profit. Be optimistic but realistic, I would say.

My prior experience with Nordstrom helped me with billiard retail as well, on follow-up of pool table deliveries, on building a general ambience in the store and good customer service. Nordstrom still does things right in that capacity. Without customers, what do you have? Customers are the single greatest asset you will ever have at your business. Focus on them. Invest in them.

As I mentioned before, after I had experienced 10 years in retail, I decided to go out on my own and wholesale the many varieties of pool cues to billiard supplies and the endless number of poolrooms that opened in the late 1980s, after The Color of Money had debuted. I achieved another level of hands-on experience in running my own business and taking care of customers.

A family physician once told me, "If you own and run your own business, the 60 hours a week you put in is for yourself, at least, and that's a good feeling." I found his philosophy to be entirely accurate. This independence offered me the experience of having to make this small business work on its own. Albeit not hugely profitable, DK Cues was my first stint at being an independent entrepreneur and gave me invaluable lessons in paying bills on time and making an ample profit to pay all my business and personal expenses.

*Brian Fairley, always willing to help with info about the bar business.*

Around 1980 I met bar owner Brian Fairly, who was proprietor of Brian's Beer and Billiards in Fullerton. I sold Brian his pool tables, which are still there today, and I became a regular customer of his for years to come. He was always very helpful with any questions I had about the bar business, and even loaned me a business proposal he had used as a template to open his business. I acknowledged my lack of experience in the bar business, and I was hungry to learn how to make a bar successful. Brian's bar was one of the most successful in Orange County, and so I knew I was asking questions and gleaning information from the right person.

On a few occasions, Brian and I attempted to open a business together. Even though Danny O'Brian's never opened, the experience helped season me to become a bar owner. Getting to know the right people and asking the right questions before you open your doors for business is invaluable to the success of your operation. And usually the cost is only that of a few beers! I found that spending money in an entrepreneur's place of business makes that person much friendlier when you inquire about the nature of his operation. I am an open book for anyone who wants to ask me about how to start up a similar operation (in fact, I am writing a book about it!).

While we were in the planning stages of opening Danny O'Brian's, part of our strategy was for me to work as a bar manager at Brian's Beer and Billiards to learn the bar trade. This gave me the hands-on experience of pouring beer, serving food, using the cash register, and managing employees for our impending operation. I learned and incorporated the philosophy of "quick, friendly service" at Danny K's when it finally opened.

Even with the knowledge I had obtained from working in the billiard industry and from Brian's Bar, I wasn't prepared enough for what I was about to experience in opening such a large endeavor as Danny K's.

Because I could not predict how busy we would be after opening, I hired three managers with different types of experience to cover shifts, make schedules, operate the main computer upstairs, order food, liquor, paper goods, beer, and so forth, and to control the throng of people I envisioned visiting and enjoying my room.

Each and every manager assured me that I needed to do nothing, that they would take care of the entire operation. I soon found out that, for one thing, I couldn't afford three managers, and that they seemed to resent me for not coming in and taking charge. And we all could see the writing on the wall: Danny K's was going to struggle to stay open, and personnel needed to go.

One night, after being open for a couple of months, as I was sitting having dinner on our main stage area, I noticed that waitresses were walking right by without serving me. The managers had convinced me that I should not correct the waitresses as it was better if they would handle the management of wait staff, so I called the general manager to complain. He became defensive and suggested that I shouldn't hurt the waitresses' feelings, that they had to have good self-esteem to give good service. This incident spelled the end for the general manager. Within a few months, all the managers were gone. Good customer service to everyone is not an option but a necessity. All the managers did their best, and all made their contribution to Danny K's. They had devised and instituted a protocol for daily operations, some of which we use today. But it was time for me to step in, and I was ready and eager to do so.

It was a difficult transition. The managers had spoiled the waitresses to the point that I had to let go of about half of them. I did not like firing the waitresses, but I could see that we had to have a new staff whose customer service skills were aligned with what I envisioned for Danny K's. I retained those servers whom I believed could support my vision. The business always comes first! If you put being obsequious or an unwillingness to confront people first, the business will suffer.

It could be argued that I should have been more experienced before opening Danny K's, and I wouldn't disagree. However, the ideal of a perfectly prepared first-time business owner is perhaps an unrealistic expectation. It's impossible to anticipate the many facets of opening a business of this size, and much of the job must be learned while working in the trenches. In my defense, I was still building the physical structure of the business when we opened, and needed the extra help for opening and continued operation.

In retrospect, having the managers to run operations on the ground was probably necessary and helpful until I could get my feet wet and learn the countless aspects needed to run the business efficiently. I was still a work in progress, and I was making one mistake after another. We are all human and are going to make mistakes, pretty much every day. Opening a new business is inviting mistakes to come in and teach you, if you're willing and able to learn.

Just after we opened Danny K's, the food would often come out burnt or cold. And so I needed to learn the menu in its entirety, and I cooked a few lunches myself just to learn how the meals needed to be prepared and presented to our clientele. This also gave me a better perspective on how the cooks dealt with servers, since I was then also dealing with them on a daily basis.

I can say that I have worked every job at Danny K's. It's important to have that perspective of what your employees do every day. This way you can correct them in the right way when necessary. A good owner takes the time to learn every job. It enables us to understand what each employee goes through, and what to expect from them. And they will respect us more because we have done their job.

I want to discuss the benefit of a good education when running a small business. Even though I did not pursue a career in psychology after I earned my degrees, the years in school unexpectedly taught me how to use formulas to calculate profit/loss percentages, how to write an important letter to the landlord or to the city, how to think more philosophically about seemingly catastrophic situations, and so on. Even earning an Associate of Arts degree at a community college is helpful in bestowing confidence. The ability to think abstractly and creatively is an asset that will help you to keep up with the competition and discover avenues for making a profit.

Also, I learned throughout the years that many people have talents that I don't necessarily have. This is a revelation that I think takes a long time for many of us to truly grasp, and it is a vital understanding for a successful business. Maybe I am a very good people person. I can read people, have become very comfortable around them, and know how to make them feel comfortable. This is one of my assets. Other people have qualities that I don't have; for instance, bartending. I don't really enjoy dealing with the public that way day in and day out. And so I have hired really good bartenders who enjoy this position, and who do much better than I would behind the bar. And my GM, Jami Jun, is very good with electronics, including TVs and the POS system. I appreciate his abilities and reward him for these.

Giving others credit for being good at what they do is a smart and humble way in which to manage a good-sized business. The number one priority is that the business is successful, no matter how that is done (as long as it is legal and moral), so being selfless, and acknowledging and respecting someone else's abilities is a complimentary asset.

On-the-job training is something that we all experience when opening a business. However, the less on-the-job training we have to do, the more likely the business will be successful. So do your homework and get the proper amount of training you feel is necessary before venturing out on your own. In the end, you will appreciate the effort you made in gaining the necessary amount of experience. It's time well spent in making your dream business a reality.

# FINDING A LOCATION

A good location is important, though it may not be the most important aspect of opening this type of operation. The better the location, the more expensive the monthly rent. A center that already has an anchor store, such as a supermarket chain or major department store, is unlikely to lease to a billiard room/ sports bar because that particular store probably has a clause in their lease to exclude any businesses that they would deem detrimental to their type of operation.

A good location for a destination-type business such as a billiard room should be close to an interstate freeway or major avenues, because customers will travel from a 20-mile radius to enjoy their sport. My room is within three miles of five different freeways and is three blocks away from one. Even though my location seems a bit hidden from most major streets, the rent is good for that reason, and being freeway-close makes up for the obscure location.

Any new business needs time to get its feet firmly on the ground, and a heavy lease payment in the beginning can feel like an anchor around one's neck. Rents today (in Southern California) are in the $2.25 to $3.00 (triple net) per square foot per month range. For a 10,000-square-foot building like Danny K's, the cost can be devastating. Most poolrooms or sports bars can open with a significantly smaller space. If I opened another Danny K's, I think I could do it with about 7,000 square feet. This difference in square footage would allow for a better location and would see savings on maintenance, air conditioning, and overhead.

A poolroom, bar, or sports bar attempting to open inside a major metropolitan area will probably need to obtain a conditional use permit to be allowed to operate within that city. Most businesses can open without a CUP; however, for good reason, the city fathers make sure that the bar or poolroom owners in their city are going to run a clean, responsible operation that will benefit the city and area.

Most cities do not want another bar in their community. They will usually object and make it difficult for any place serving alcohol (that is not a restaurant), and offering pool tables. Poolrooms have never been popular in metropolitan areas. Therefore, it is important to go into the planning department prepared with a complete plan of action to display how your operation will benefit the city.

After entertaining about a dozen or so spaces for a sports bar/ billiard room, I narrowed my search by excluding several types of locations. First of all, if the space is within 500 feet of a church or school, most cities will not allow this kind of business to open in that location. If parking is sparse, the city is unlikely to allow it as well. Generally, a sports bar/billiard room/restaurant will need to have the same parking restrictions as a regular restaurant, which usually mandates about eight spaces per thousand square feet. A 5,000-square-foot business would have to have 40 parking spaces for itself. And, you'll need to have those parking spots on a Friday or Saturday night when business is booming.

My first step was to call the city and get a general attitude or feeling from the planning department about my type of operation in the location I like for my business. If their attitude was negative, I chucked the idea of a room in that spot. If their view was positive, I might go to the next step of calling the police department. If the police department had no problem with the location, I would call the Alcohol Beverage Control and inquire about the possibilities of acquiring a beer and wine and liquor license in that area. The ABC will not issue a license where there are many licenses in a certain confined area. For instance, if there are three or four liquor licenses within a city block, they will be reluctant to issue another one in that specific area. If their attitude is negative, then that is reason enough to scrap that location. Fighting city hall, the local police, or the ABC is usually an exercise in futility. Save your time, energy, and mental health, and find another space.

My experience in Orange County, dealing with planning departments of several cities was a positive one overall. I was always upbeat and patient, and grateful for any information I could obtain. And of course they were usually appreciative of my good attitude. I know of a man who constantly gave the city a hard time. He managed to get a business open, but after an intense fight to win that victory, he did not have a good relationship with the city. Not ideal.

All of the cities where I inquired about opening a place mandated that notifications of my type of business opening in a designated spot were sent out within a 300-foot radius of the location. If there were several residential homes within that radius, then I could expect objections from the homeowners. Homeowners fear a bad crowd coming into a bar and pool room, and usually feel that such an establishment can negatively affect the neighborhood. So the city is doing the proper thing in sending out notices to local residences.

Before I opened Danny K's, I had a friend who tried to open a poolroom and bar within a few hundred feet of some expensive homes in the City of Orange. He asked me to come and speak on his behalf to convince the planning commission to approve his opening. I noticed 20 or so local residents sitting in the front row ready to argue against his opening. I knew right away he had no chance. I was correct. They voted 5 to 0 to deny his business opening at that location. These residents are constituents of the members of the planning commission and of the city council. If enough of them object, the chances of opening will not be good. The city fathers must act at the behest of their constituents, or they won't be re-elected! Residents' opinions hold a lot of power.

I discovered the room for Danny K's in an industrial area that had no residential homes. To boot, the nearest church was over a thousand feet away. Also, there was no school nearby. The location had housed a Gold's Gym in 1985 when I noticed it, and the only residents nearby were people temporarily living in a motor home park to the west side of the building. There were 90 parking spots for the 10,000-square-foot building. I knew that city requirements for my type of business would necessitate eight parking spaces for every 1,000 square feet, so we were fine with the amount of parking there.

*Danny K's had been a gym, and we were lucky to be able to use the existing restrooms.*

I knew the rent would be reasonable, because of the industrial proximity of the building. Industrial and manufacturing properties are usually cheaper than commercial or retail, because of parking availability and proximity of the space in relation to major arteries and visibility, etc. And so, when the building came up for lease in about 1992, I pursued it as a possible location for my business.

I called the City of Orange and inquired about a billiard room/restaurant/sports bar in that location. I let them know upfront that it would be an upscale place, catering to middle- and upper-class adults, and would be well-managed and operated. Their response was initially positive with reservations, and I set out to show them how this business would be a benefit to the city. I received a similar reaction from the police department and the Alcohol Beverage Control Board. It was my job then to prove to them that my place would create no new problems for the area.

I had a go-ahead from all the agencies that could possibly nix my dream; my next step was to contact the leasing agent for the building. The leasing agent representing the landlord was a little surprised with the idea I had for the building. Nevertheless, he contacted the owners of the property and let them know of my plans. They were skeptical but open to hearing my idea, and so I presented the leasing agent my layout of the place along with a business proposal and ideas for the operation, and he relayed them to the landlord.

The landlord was a middle-aged woman, and her father and uncle owned the building. Even though they were taken aback by the proposed use of the building, we convinced them that our business would be exceptional for this type of use. They reluctantly gave us a shot. And, with the exception of the first year in business, they have not regretted it. Twenty-five years later, they have made a few million off of my business. And I am happy for them. I have attempted to purchase the property a few times, but it is not and never will be for sale. Everyone is happy, and it is a win-win for all.

My partner and I gave the owners a non-refundable security deposit of $5,000, and our next move was a CUP (Conditional Use Permit) hearing with the City of Orange. The city planning commission is usually made up of elected officials that will approve certain city uses if the proposed use comports with the rules already in the city charter. Poolrooms and bars need a CUP in order to get permission to open in most cities. The City of Orange had five members who sat on the planning commission in 1993. If the planning commission does not approve your application, then it is usually referred to the city council, which is higher up on the totem pole of the city. The mayor is head of the city council.

I made copies of all the homework I'd done on research of billiard rooms, pictures of higher-class places like mine nearby and in other states, and even presented part of my business plan to show how dedicated I was to running a nice establishment. All planning commission members received a nice folder ahead of time that I had made personally for them that included all this information. When I went before the planning commission board in the summer of 1993, the strongest enemy I had to fight was my own anxiety. It seemed like a life-or-death situation for me at the time, because I had invested so much of my life into my dream.

When I peered up at the panel and saw all smiles, I knew I had succeeded in winning them over before I had spoken a word. One planning commission member even stated she would enjoy coming in after it opened. And I can say this; I proved them correct in their decision. Danny K's has been a benefit to the community, by offering a place for regular adult citizens of the City of Orange to enjoy the hobby of pool, good food, and a myriad of sporting events while imbibing the beverage of their choice. Luckily for me the city was not doing well financially and needed the revenue obtained by the taxes we would be paying.

In short, the location should be a reasonable choice, one that the city is ready to allow and that the police can rest assured that they won't be encumbering a new headache. The way to satisfy these conditions is to call all local agencies that will have a decision-making impact on your business. If you have serious doubts about the city, the police department, or the ABC approving your proposal, I suggest moving on to another possible location.

Your lease for the site should be of major financial concern. Especially in the very beginning when money may be tight, a huge rent payment can push you to the cusp of financial ruin. That is why the best location may not be the right one for your particular vision.

Some of the locations I looked into were large enough, but the rent would have been astronomical, and I didn't feel that I could have generated the amount of income needed to keep the place open and realize a tidy profit. I would discount these types of locations.

*The original awning we had made in the mid 90's.*

Most rents in strip malls that are centrally located are high and have a triple net addition per month. This triple net means that you will share maintenance of the building(s) and parking lot with the other tenants. It also means that you share in the cost of building insurance and property taxes. These costs can add as much as 15 to 20 percent to your monthly rent. So if your rent per month is $15,000, the triple net fee will be another $2,500 or $3,000. It's a way for the landlord to offer the site at a smaller price per square foot. Still, it is a part of the lease and will need to be paid.

One reason I scoped out the site for Danny K's and decided it would be satisfactory from early on was that I figured the rent would be reasonable. The building was, and still is, mostly in an industrial area where many businesses are doing light manufacturing or have small service businesses. So I knew that we would have time to grow while building the business. Finding a location like Danny K's is not easy in the current market.

We were paying in the neighborhood of 59 cents a square foot with no triple net charge when we opened. This was higher than any of the gyms before us had paid. Once we began to thrive, the rent was raised every chance the landlord was able to do so. We now pay triple that original amount and all the expenses as well for maintenance, taxes, and insurance. I am okay with it. The landlord is doing well, and so are we.

The building has been part of a family trust, and has never been for sale. The landlord has assured me that if they do sell the building I will be the first to know and will have the option to purchase. Purchasing the building is a good idea for any business owner, because your monthly payments go into equity on the property. This is not always an option or realistic for most businesses though.

Usually the asking rent for most places can be negotiated. If the commercial real estate that you are inquiring about is busy all the time and the spots are always occupied, you may need to pay the asking rate. If the economy is booming and all stores in the center are taken, it is likely that this will be the case. In a downturn, though, and if several stores are empty, you can offer significantly less than the asking price. I suggest that you offer a minimum amount and then negotiate a price that both the landlord and you are happy with.

In the early 90s, a billiard room opened in a very expensive area in Huntington Beach. I can't remember the name of the place, but it was near the ocean, had a nice deli, a beautiful bar, and expensive fixtures and pool tables. This 7,000-square-foot location was paying $25,000 per month triple net. This amounted to about $4 per square foot. They just couldn't make enough money out of the room to recognize a decent profit. After a few years they had to close down. The lesson here is to be careful and frugal concerning the amount of your lease. Rents at certain levels can make even profitable businesses unsustainable.

Once you are open in your new location, it is important to build the place out and open for business as soon as possible. Every day that you're not in business is a day you're not making money to pay rent. In most places nowadays, with the rent and other expenses due every month and with no income coming into the business it can become very stressful. It took Danny K's six months to open once we secured the building and signed the lease, and if you are on a budget like we were this is a long time.

*We were able to afford this sign after a couple of years. We change the marquee every week.*

Some landlords who are in need of a tenant will offer free rent for a few months, or even cash to help you get open. If they feel that you will be a reliable tenant for many years, then it behooves them to help you open your business. This is not typical, though it is possible.

The term of the lease should be of a duration that gives you a chance to begin making and sustaining a significant profit. Most leases in today's market are five years with an option for another five. This way, after the first five years if the business isn't doing well and you decide to close it down you are not obligated for the remainder of a much longer lease. We opened with a 10-year lease with percentages of increase each year. Since then we have been on a five-year lease with a five-year option.

Be careful and read every part of your lease. Most leases require that you begin negotiating with the landlord six months before the lease runs out. If you fail to do so, it can invalidate the upcoming five-year option. If you feel that you cannot quite understand the legal terms of the lease, I suggest you have an attorney review it with you and explain the details.

Renewing the lease and negotiating increases are very important. In a good economy, increases are a matter of course. The amount of increase is critical. If your rent significantly increases, you may need to raise prices commensurately to pay for that extra monthly payment. Increases in your prices will not always be popular with your regular customers. Generally, the landlord will want you to stay, and will be amenable to negotiating a fair increase in rent. During a significant downturn in the economy, as in the 2008 recession, you can ask for a decrease in rent. I asked for a decrease in rent, the landlord assented, and it was reduced by about 10%. Always ask for any possible benefits the landlord may give you. It never hurts to ask.

The location and lease are major concerns of any small business. Be diligent, find the best possible location at the best rent, and sign a lease that is reasonable and will allow you to sustain a healthy income for years in the future.

# PARTNERSHIP AGREEMENT

A good and complete partnership agreement is critical whether you have several investors or only one partner. One of the best attorneys I know had a saying in quotes above his door, "Let us put this agreement in pen, so that we will be friends to the end." With everything in writing, disputes are settled simply by reviewing the agreement.

A partnership agreement spells out specific duties by individual partners. Since my partnership was with one person and involved a 50/50 split on everything in the business, we had our own duties and responsibilities defined by the agreement. Because this was my dream and I presumed to know what I was doing in running Danny K's, I was labeled the operations manager by the agreement. My responsibilities involved managing employees, marketing, and everyday operations that would make Danny K's a successful endeavor. And I was expected to work more hours and to be given a higher salary than my partner.

The partnership agreement also indicated the amount of contributions from each individual. If more money is contributed later, the agreement can be amended. Our agreement indicated that my partner was to contribute 90 percent of all moneys, and I would contribute 10 percent. As it worked out, I probably contributed a little more than that because of leases I signed for the music and TV system, but my partner was able to get other parties to loan us money, so it all worked out in the end.

My partner was 20 years older than I, nearing retirement, and not nearly as familiar as I was with this type of operation, so his responsibilities entailed repairs and maintenance, and required fewer hours per week. He would also do the daily sales report before we opened every day and make deposits. Over the years, he excelled in performing to his job description, and when he retired in 2006 we left on very good terms, and he received a nice buyout package. It was not all rosy, especially in the beginning, but as Shakespeare said, "All's well that ends well."

There are other issues covered by a partnership agreement that are critical. My partner had another business that was in operation at the time we opened. It began to flounder, and he was concerned that it might go under. It finally did go under, and after looking at the monthly balance sheet, I noticed that we owed more money than the previous month. I confronted my partner, and he indicated that those were moneys owed from his other business. He had transferred the credit card debt from his failed business to ours. He thought this was okay, because he had funded most of Danny K's.

I immediately showed him in the partnership agreement where this was not allowed, and he subsequently took off the debt and paid it himself. I can't really blame him for attaching the debt, since he had always been an individual owner and never had a partner. It would have been natural to put the debt onto this business had he been a sole owner. But now this did not work, of course. The partnership agreement spelled out that the "acquiring of debt that is not agreed to by both partners" was not allowed. No one was resentful over this. Everything we put in writing did its job.

The agreement will also spell out how much time each partner is required to spend in the business. For example, it may state that one partner may not be able to moonlight doing a similar job somewhere else, which may detract from his duties at the business. If one of the partners is designated as only working part time, then the agreement may indicate that he or she can work another job. Partners generally will contribute different assets to a business, some monetary and others experience. Again, it's important to spell these responsibilities out so the partnership agreement can be used as a guide and arbiter in case of a disagreement.

The agreement will also indicate what will be done in the event that someone dies or becomes disabled, or if a partner desires for his part to be bought out. In my partner's case, he decided to retire at 75 when he did not want to continue the day-to-day duties that the partnership agreement had spelled out for him. So we came up with a figure that was agreeable to both of us, and I was able to pay him off in about eight years. That is why I say that the partnership agreement is critical, and not just necessary.

What if a partner wants to sell his or her ownership of the business? Our agreement stated that the remaining partner had the right to purchase that share of the business at the same price offered to a possible incoming partner. This makes sense, because partnerships are like marriages in a way. You may not care for the person who wants to buy your partner out. Plus, this option can give you an opportunity to own the business outright.

If there is a major dispute, the partnership agreement will indicate the manner in which the dispute will be settled, usually through mediation or arbitration. Our agreement stated arbitration, which is more complex and costly than mediation. Arbitration is less formal than a trial, but involves a judge and testimony. Mediation is a process of negotiation with the assistance of a neutral third party. In mediation, a resolution is not met until all parties agree. If the partners want to remain civil during the course of their partnership,

I recommend mediation. Hopefully the partnership never comes to this point.

When the business is ready to be closed or goes under, there should be a clause for dissolution. This will indicate what will happen once the business has closed, so all persons are treated fairly, in accordance with what was decided by all and placed into the agreement. This will minimize conflicts between partners at the end of the life of the business.

I recommend you pay an attorney to write up an agreement that will cover all contingencies that may arise during the course of business. If you absolutely cannot afford to have an attorney draw one up, there are templates on the web that you can follow. If you go this route, spend the time and make sure all bases are covered.

I was very lucky to have an honest partner who was amenable to my way of operating Danny K's, but not all people are like my partner was. What if your partner disagrees with your manner of operating the business? Or what if your partner tries to embezzle money or add debt to the business? With a good, comprehensive partnership agreement, everyone's interests are protected and the law will be on your side.

# FORMULATING A
# BUSINESS PROPOSAL

A business proposal should be a template and guide for the opening and continued successful operation of your endeavor. Who, what, when, where, why, and how are necessary questions to ask and answer in an outline form for initial and continued reference. Even if you don't refer back to the business proposal after you've opened your doors, creating it and working on it as a matter of discipline can help you to discover and remember the many facets of operating a business of this nature. The business proposal is also necessary in procuring a potential business partner (or partners) or in borrowing necessary capital from any lending institution.

I also included my business proposal in the portfolio I gave to the city planning commission. The outline of what I wanted to do showed my seriousness about the venture and the professional intent for its continued operation. Since almost all cities are leery of billiard rooms and bars opening in their vicinity, a complete account of what you plan to do can help persuade the city to consider your operation over the many others that don't appear to have prepared to deal with the negative image that opening a pool room can portray.

You can find many good templates for small business proposals in a local library, bookstore, or online. I was lucky enough to be offered a plan from someone who already had a similar and successful operation. Brian Fairley unselfishly loaned me his business proposal, and I used his as a template for Danny K's.

The plan should create excitement as well as cover all aspects of opening and then operating your business. The first page might be one that summarizes your lifelong dream and the profit you plan on making. It can include much of your personal experience and the passion you have to make your dream work. How is this business going to be exceptional compared to similar operations in the county? What kind of operation is it? Is it going to focus more on pool, sports, food or beverages? The introduction in a business proposal is like a hook that encourages the reader to continue. It doesn't have to be long, just engaging and to the point.

The opening segment of my plan (following the introduction) was entitled, "Theme and Atmosphere." What will it feel like to enter your business? When a person enters for the first time, how is the experience different from entering any other operation? How do the colors and furniture make the customers feel? Are the servers always friendly and smiling? Does the manager or owner shake hands and remember names? Some bar customers spend much of their lives patronizing a local hangout—is yours a place where they will feel welcome and want to return? How is the lighting, and what wall hangings or pictures will you use? How many pool tables do you plan on including? What about darts, shuffleboard, foosball, or video games? The "Theme and Atmosphere" segment for my proposal gave the reader a look at the inside of Danny K's, before it was even open.

And then you might follow your "Theme and Atmosphere" statement with a pro forma income statement, or a prediction of how well your business will do financially after opening. The pro forma income statement should show all fixed expenses per month, such as rent, utilities (even though they will vary some), liability, worker's comp insurance, or any other expenses you expect to be fairly consistent every month. The other constants in monthly expenses are likely more variable from month to month, such as payroll, cost of goods, needed repairs, upgrades, and so on.

After listing expenses, you then indicate your expected monthly gross sales. This should be optimistic, but realistic. Why should someone invest in a plan that isn't going to show a healthy gross income and net profit?

Again, if you search your local library or search the web you'll find a workable template for a good business proposal. If you can find a template that resonates with your taste, then that may be the one you should use.

The summary for a business plan should be a synopsis of your dream business, and how you are going to bring this dream to fruition. It should inspire enthusiasm and excitement. The reader might review it and think, "I'd like to be a part of this."

Acquiring enough capital for opening this type of operation can be the major stumbling block in opening your business. Not everyone will be as willing to invest in your dream as you are. Convincing prospective investors should be as much a priority as choosing your location and the methods for running your business.

In the business proposal, you must estimate the necessary funding to open the operation of your dream. You can add at least 20 percent to that total for unexpected opening expenses. And that percentage is about right if you considered anything and everything needed to open.

Here is a sample of an outline I used in opening Danny K's:

## MISSION STATEMENT

The heading for this page can be your logo, or the name of your business. It can begin by stating what you are proposing and what kind of impact it will have on the community and on investors.

Something like, "In the many years of searching for a sports bar and billiard room location, we have found a site that is ideal for this dream to see reality." It should intrigue anyone reading it, so they want to reading further.

Your mission statement should state your vision, the reason why you are opening this operation. Why do you have a passion for this business? How long have you dreamed of doing this and thought about what it will eventually be like? And what kind of profit can an investor expect to share in with you and any other partner(s)?

The statement should also reveal some of your background that has prepared you for managing this type of operation in this particular industry. Have you worked as a bartender, and you know how the bar industry works from the inside? Do you have any kitchen experience?

In my case, I had years of billiards experience, having been a professional pool player and having worked in the retail and wholesale end of billiard sales. These experiences were not necessarily specific to operating a billiard room, but I had been around and played in enough poolrooms to understand how they operated and the profit they would potentially realize. I knew what customers would want. I had also worked in a bar as a manager for a while, and my experience with retail sales demonstrated my knowledge in the matter of making a profit after costs and expenses.

However large or small your previous experience in your preferred business is, spelling out the applicable experience in a brief mission statement is extremely important. The potential investor or planning commission will review this statement against business viability and how it will perform on an ongoing basis. The leaser will also check your statement in terms of the possibility of long-term success to confirm that the tenant will be leasing for a continued duration.

The mission statement is the initial hook that potential investors read and become excited, or at least intrigued, by what this proposal represents. What sets your business apart from the others in your area? How are you going to operate this sports bar and restaurant to stand out from those that investors have visited in the past? This statement presents the "WOW" factor.

And when you look back on this mission statement after years of operation, you can track your progress—how closely and well you've followed your mission. It is a good reminder of what you planned and how much has come to fruition.

## THEME AND ATMOSPHERE

Now you present the details of how it feels to enter this dream location. The theme and atmosphere should describe what customers experience when they enter your place. This section should also be interesting and alluring to the reader.

What will your place be like, according to your dream? What kinds of food and drink will you serve? And the ambience—how will the atmosphere be better than the sports bar and billiard room a few miles away? Are the pool tables professional models? Is the lighting above the tables conducive to patrons returning to play? Do you plan on implementing a specific style throughout the place?

Will the flooring be carpet, tile, or wood? And how will the flooring complement the pool tables and wall decor? What about architectural details, such as crown molding bordering your room? What about the wall paint color and decor? Even the ceiling color or treatment is important. We have deep red walls, a rose-colored crown molding and a forest green ceiling. The color of the ceiling reflects the color of the cloth of the pool tables, emphasizing the main attraction of the establishment. The deep red, warm green, and woody brown that feature throughout Danny K's are colors that I personally like, and my customers do as well. The color scheme was popular in the 80's, and it has aged well because it took its inspiration from the pool tables themselves. The overall effect creates an inviting, vintage-inspired atmosphere. Every space has its own physical limitations, assets, and basic characteristics. Mine is very large with very high ceilings, and I worked within those parameters to create an ambience that feels both cozy and spacious.

At Danny K's we have photos of actors and actresses playing pool on the walls, mostly in movie scenes they have performed in. And then there are some sports photos, and a host of beer neons below the crown molding. The neons were a relatively inexpensive decoration, since most beer distributors donate them for their own advertising, and since we have 33 beers on tap, they are well represented by the neon signs.

Is your service going to be the best in the area? How is your service going to be set apart from other bars in the county? You can easily write a full page on your establishment's theme and atmosphere. This is where you can really sell your dream by painting a clear picture!

## BUSINESS LAYOUT

This page of your business proposal gives the reader a diagram and bird's-eye view of what your place will look like. It is essentially a blueprint that shows where the bar is located, the location of walk-in coolers, restrooms, kitchen (and equipment), hallways (if any), pub tables and bar stools, TVs and pool tables, if you intend to include a pool room, etc.

It is important to check with your local city building and health departments so you can conform to whatever codes they have for restrooms, kitchens, walkways, etc. For instance, every walkway to an exit has to have a minimum of six feet clearance per the City of Orange, where Danny K's is located. And when we opened, the inspector confirmed on the final sign-off we obtained that we had a minimum of six feet of space leading to an exit. These inspectors will do their job in accordance with regulations set down by the city building department, with no exceptions or shortcuts.

*The large room at Danny K's when it was a gym. Originally it was our main entrance.*

There are many details to consider for the physical elements of the building. The number of drains needed in the kitchen and bar is important to research. Sinks, coolers, freezers, fryers, broiler, griddle, pizza oven, and drink wells should be displayed in the blueprint, and the position of each must be well thought out. The hood and Ansul system in the kitchen is very important. These will all be inspected by the health department after they are installed and approved.

I made numerous visits to the Orange County Health Department and the City of Orange so that I could comply with the many details and demands required by both institutions. You can highlight all of these requirements in your layout, so that people reading the proposal understand that you have done your research. This will also make you more familiar with the layout of the place, in case there is a clogged drain, problem with the hood, or other difficulties. You should know every bit of your place inside and out, and writing the business layout will get you there.

*The Men's restroom and eventual walk-in cooler and bar. We used every existing fixture we could, including toilets and partitions. The men's shower became the walk-in.*

When you are designing your room, unless you have unlimited funds, it is important to use the facilities as they are already situated in your space. If you can use existing restrooms but modify them, you save time and money. Of course, contact the city and health department regarding the restrooms. The size of the handicapped toilet and restrictions of space here and there are very important. Many lawsuits by handicapped people happened in Orange County a few years ago, because restaurants did not have the correct handicapped restroom stall. Again, the health department and city building department will typically inspect these before you can open, so comply as well as you can.

Since the bar will need plumbing, placing the bar adjacent to the restrooms is usually a good idea. If the kitchen is nearby, that is a benefit as well. Connecting the bulk of the plumbing this way makes building configurations and maintenance easier and less expensive. You can also highlight this in the layout—kitchen, restrooms, and bar close together, and all using the same plumbing lines. It will save time, money, and future plumbing expenses.

*The men's shower that was in the gym. We walled it in and created a walk-in cooler*

Since my billiards room had been a Gold's Gym, the restrooms were already basically there as part of the men's and women's locker rooms. The restrooms only needed to be walled in and remodeled. On the men's side I connected the plumbing to the bar and built it in that area. I then left a passageway from the bar to the nearby wall for customer traffic to go from one side of Danny K's to the other. We were short on money, and this was really the only way we could realistically build it out. The men's shower was adjacent to the men's restroom, and was a perfect location for the walk-in cooler, being also adjacent to the bar. Now we have 33 beers on tap connected directly to the walk-in, not underground beer lines or beer coolers under the taps. While these alternatives can work, it is much better to have a walk-in that butts up to the back bar.

*The original women's restroom and locker room. The excess space after a wall became the kitchen.*

On the women's locker room side, we walled in the women's restroom, using the existing plumbing, and just connected the sinks with pipes when we built the kitchen from the remainder of the women's restroom space. They've been operable for the past 24 years. The women's restroom is a little large considering most of our customers are male, but our female customers appreciate the space.

The layout for Danny K's may not have been ideal compared to what I initially wanted; however, using the features already present in the building saved a lot of time and money, and that value cannot be overstated. I saved approximately a $100,000 by not demolishing everything and beginning anew. And it worked out well. Using the original restrooms split the space up so that it is not just one huge room, and the floor plan also offers different areas for private parties. It makes for a more interesting place, for sure.

The layout should also show distances from one pool table to another, how far the bar is away from the back bar or any auxiliary bars you might have, and the size and distances between the pub tables. Also, the actual sizes of the pool tables are important when configuring a layout, because every square inch is vital when someone is shooting a shot off the rail and extending the pool cue over another pool table.

These distances referenced in your layout gives the reader a clear perspective of what you want to do and shows you've done your homework, adding to your credibility when asking investors for money.

## PRO FORMA INCOME STATEMENT

A major hurdle for opening a business can be acquiring enough capital. Those who are looking to invest may not initially share your vision or your dream. In the end, it's critical that investors believe in your dream, even if it is not their own. Convincing prospective investors of the value and potential of your vision should be of utmost importance, since without capital, you can't get open.

In presenting a pro forma income statement, you are showing prospective partners the amount of net profit you will eventually earn on a consistent basis. It should be a realistic indication of what will occur after the business opens, and use evidence to back up your numbers. It should be optimistic and reflect a strong volume and solid net profit. Investors will want to see consistent long-term profit. What follows is only a moderate opening estimate and in no way reflects what Danny K's income is per month.

## Pro Forma Income Statement:

| Estimated income: | Monthly | Yearly |
|---|---|---|
| Beer sales (draft) | $30,000 | $360,000 |
| Liquor | $25,000 | $300,000 |
| Food | $18,000 | $216,000 |
| Billiards | $12,000 | $144,000 |
| Beer sales (bottled) | $10,000 | $120,000 |
| Non Alcohol | $9,000 | $98,000 |
| Wine | $6,000 | $72,000 |
| Misc. (shirt sales, magazines, etc.) | $5,000 | $60,000 |
| Totals | $115,000 | $1,380,000 |

| Cost of Goods: | Monthly | Yearly |
|---|---|---|
| Draft Beer | $7,800 | $93,600 |
| Liquor | $4,500 | $54,000 |
| Food | $6,660 | $79,920 |
| Bottled beer | $2,500 | $30,000 |
| Non Alcohol | $2,250 | $27,000 |
| Wine | $1,800 | $21,600 |
| Misc. | $2,500 | $30,000 |
| Cost of Goods Total | $28,010 | $336,120 |

**Gross Profit:**   $115,000−$28,010=86,990   12×86,990 = $1,043,880

And so you can see the gross profit is generally very good. Now it's time to figure monthly operating expenses. It is extremely important to keep operating expenses to a minimum without cutting back on customer service and customer comfort. The restaurant and bar industry, unlike retail sales, works on a higher gross profit, but will incur higher labor costs, due to food and drink preparation and service. Keeping payroll at a minimum is really important.

Expenses are categorized as fixed and variable. Simply put, costs that remain consistent (mostly) each month are fixed, and those that will vary are variable.

### Fixed costs per month:

| | |
|---|---|
| Rent | $12,000 |
| Bookkeeping | $600 |
| Towel service | $800 |
| Pest control | $400 |
| Hood cleaning | $200 |
| Filter replacement | $200 |
| Insurance (Workers Comp, Liability) | $3,500 |
| **Total** | **$19,100** |

Liability insurance will be required by the landlord, and worker's comp is required by state law. In any case, search until you can find the cheapest of both of these. I have two insurance agents I work with. They don't particularly like having someone else to bid against, but this keeps the price down for me. And they usually both make money. I choose not to buy employee practices liability insurance, even though many places do purchase it. I do my best to make sure everyone takes their breaks and also make sure that I have an open door if an employee feels compromised in any way, physically or emotionally.

# Variable cost per month:

Payroll          $30,000

*(Usually an average of 30% of gross sales. As long as the owner operates his own place, which I recommend in the beginning, this cost will be considerably less.)*

Utilities          $5,000

*(Will vary from summer to winter. A/C is by far the highest cost here. Electrical, telephone, water, gas, etc.)*

Repairs and maintenance (includes pool    $8,000
table recoveries and billiard upkeep. Also
A/C repair, kitchen, bar, and poolroom
maintenance and repair)

| | |
|---|---|
| Advertising & Promotion | $1,000 |
| Utilities | $5,000 |
| Credit Card Discount (CC cost) | $1,100 |
| Telephone | $1,200 |
| Kitchen Supplies | $1,500 |
| Legal | $500 |
| Security | $400 |
| Equipment Rental | $200 |
| Paper/Sanitary Supplies | $150 |

**Total: $53,050 monthly**

Fixed Costs + Variable Costs:

**$72,150 monthly**

Yearly Totals:          $72,150 x 12 = $865,800
per year

Gross profit per year less costs:       $1,043,880 – $865,800

(Net Profit) $178,080

Net Profit as a percent of Gross Sales: $178,080 - $1,380,000 = 13% (Net Profit)

Note that as your gross sales go up, your percentage of net profit will go up as well. If, for example, you achieve a $2,000,000 per year gross sales figure, your net profit may grow from 15 to 20 percent. The reason for this is that your costs will not go up commensurate with your gross sales. While everything, including payroll, will increase some, the net profit will be a higher percentage. The cost of goods as a percentage of sales should always be tracked so that you maximize every bit of gross profit.

As a percent of sales,

| | |
|---|---|
| Draft beer pour cost and bottled beer cost: | 22% |
| Liquor pour cost | 16% |
| Food cost | 37% |
| Bottled beer cost | 25% |
| Non-alcohol cost | 25% |
| Wine cost | 30% |
| Misc. cost | 50% |

Notice the lower percentages of cost of sales on beer and liquor. One way to realize a good, solid net profit is to keep these costs down.

I learned that a bar in Fullerton had a combination $CO_2$ and nitrogen system for pouring beer and did my research. After determining that this could be a good idea for us, I had one installed at Danny K's. It saved 3 or 4 percent. This turned out to be a major moneymaker, because our pour cost before installing the system was an overall 31 percent (with the cost of bottled beer included).

Also, how one pours the beer can significantly decrease the size of head on the beer. Most bartenders will allow a little beer to flow out before pouring the beer into the glass. This wastes beer (and money). If the glass is placed immediately under the tap and the edge of the tap is placed on the inner side of the glass touching it, the best, most economical pour is made.

Bartenders are also not allowed to comp drinks at Danny K's, unless approved by management. I've found this to be an essential policy in keeping pour cost down. It does not deter sales at all. Most bar owners have a policy of allowing a certain amount of comps by bartenders for each shift. Unfortunately, what this does is allow a dishonest bartender to take the payment of a beer and put it in their own tip jar. Many bars are taken advantage of in this way. Customers typically just want their alcohol at a fair price. Comps are not necessary.

Liquor is lower than draft beer on the percentage of sales category, but at 16 percent cost of sales it's a moneymaker. We have yet to offer a menu on different types of drinks, but that will be forthcoming. Bartenders should make an average to healthy pour, but not over-pour. We have a responsibility to the community to make sure our customers leave Danny K's sober enough to drive. We have a very good relationship with the police department for that and other reasons.

Food cost for the industry is usually at about 33 percent. Since we use only best-quality items and keep the cost within reason for our customers, we live with a 37 percent cost. Since it's not our number one seller, we can accept a slightly higher food cost than most restaurants. It is imperative that the food always be at a high quality and prepared in an excellent way for customers. Quality counts with food.

## OPENING COST

Here are a few examples of estimated costs similar to what I used when opening Danny K's. The costs are all vague estimates, but the intent is to give you an impression of how everything needs to be spelled out so as to attract investors and convince the city of the efficacy of what you intend to do. Also, this exercise will give the business owner an estimate of the ultimate cost of opening the operation. As we mentioned earlier, opening without enough funds is a main reason why a business fails.

In calculating the ultimate cost of opening, I learned to add a percentage to all costs. A traditional rule of thumb is that the cost is usually 25% greater than what you think, and that the time frame will usually take twice as long to complete as you believe.

We opened with almost all used kitchen equipment. You can save quite a bit by purchasing used equipment. We simply did not have the money to purchase brand-new items, and most of the used equipment lasted us for several years. I recently got rid of a stove that I had for 22 years and purchased used! If you do buy new equipment, research actual costs. You may find many things online that are cheaper for the same item from a bricks-and-mortar vendor.

*Some used kitchen equipment we opened with. Most of these appliances lasted for years.*

As a general rule, you can get better deals if you purchase in volume. Buying 20 pool tables versus only buying one will give you some leverage. Always use your leverage and try to get the best deal possible. Every dollar you save in opening costs will help you survive the rough patches ahead and eventually become a sustained success.

## *BILLIARD EQUIPMENT*

| Item: | Quantity: | Price: | Total Cost: |
|---|---|---|---|
| Professional Pool Tables | 20 | $3,000 | $60,000 |
| Pool Cues and Accessories (balls, chalk, cue racks, triangles, etc.) | 20 | $200 | $4,000 |
| Pool Table Lights (six foot, oak finish, fluorescent) | 20 | $300 | $6,000 |
| Bar Stools and Seating (Darafeev stools and chairs) | 200 | $150 | $30,000 |
| Pool Ball Cleaner | 1 | $750 | $750 |
| Billiard Area Flooring | X | $25,000 | $25,000 |
| Billiard Time POS System | 1 | $3,000 | $3,000 |
| Pub Tables | 40 | $700 | $28,000 |

# KITCHEN EQUIPMENT

| Item: | Quantity: | Price: | Total Cost: |
|---|---|---|---|
| Broiler | 1 | $500 | $500 |
| Grill | 1 | $500 | $500 |
| Fryers | 2 | $600 | $1,200 |
| Pizza Oven | 1 | $600 | $600 |
| Freezers | 2 | $1,100 | $2,200 |
| Refrigerators | 2 | $1,000 | $2,000 |
| Cooler Underneath Broiler | 1 | $1,200 | $1,200 |
| Prep Coolers | 2 | $700 | $1,400 |
| Prep Tables | 3 | $600 | $1,800 |
| Dishwashing Sink | 1 | $1,500 | $1,500 |
| Misc. Racks | 4 | $500 | $2,000 |
| Kitchen Utensils | X | $4,000 | $4,000 |
| Kitchen Flooring | X | $4,000 | $4,000 |
| Drains and Walls | X | $6,000 | $6,000 |
| Food Inventory | X | $3,000 | $3,000 |

## BAR AREA

| Item: | Quantity: | Price: | Total Cost: |
|---|---|---|---|
| Walk-in Cooler | 1 | $12,000 | $12,000 |
| Back Bar | 1 | $3,000 | $3,000 |
| Main Bar | 1 | $10,000 | $10,000 |
| Under Bar Cooler | 1 | $1,500 | $1,500 |
| Beer Cooler | 1 | $1,250 | $1,250 |
| Bar Area Flooring | 1 | $6,000 | $6,000 |
| Bar Sinks/Dishwasher | 1 | $3,000 | $3,000 |
| Mixed Drink Wells | 2 | $1,000 | $2,000 |
| Liquor, Wine, Beer | X | $7,500 | $7,500 |

## RESTROOMS

| Item: | Quantity: | Price: | Total Cost: |
|---|---|---|---|
| Construction, Flooring, and Tile for Men's and Women's Restrooms | X | $25,000 | $25,000 |

## TVS AND SOUND SYSTEM

Sports bars are more popular now than when I opened Danny K's. With the glut of high-quality televisions that are available now, the expense for TVs will be much less than I experienced. The cost for a decent 55-inch TV has significantly decreased due to changes in competition and manufacturing, and hopefully the costs will remain competitive. There will be many different sizes you may use, depending on your room layout.

| Item: | Quantity: | Price: | Total Cost: |
| --- | --- | --- | --- |
| 55" TVs | 40 | $700 | $28,000 |
| 120" Projection TVs | 3 | $4,000 | $12,000 |
| Cable, TV Stands, and Installation | X | $30,000 | $30,000 |
| Amplifiers, Preamps, Speakers, Wiring, and Labor to Install | X | $30,000 | $30,000 |

## SITE REMODEL

| Item: | Cost: | Total Cost: |
| --- | --- | --- |
| Paint walls, dry wall installation, air conditioning installation, lighting, signage | $100,000 | $100,000 |

## LICENSURE

| Item: | Cost: | Total Cost: |
| --- | --- | --- |
| City Licenses (CUP and any other fees) | $2,000 | $2,000 |
| Beer and Wine License | $4,000 | $4,000 |
| ABC Liquor License | $70,000 | $70,000 |

| | |
| --- | --- |
| **Total estimated expense** | **$532,200** |
| **Add 20% (unexpected expenses)** | **$106,440** |
| **Total adjusted estimated expense** | **$639,640** |

This should give you an example of the types of total expenses you will have in opening a sports bar and billiard room. These are only estimates; depending on what type of establishment you wish to have, the costs can be considerably higher, and in some cases lower than what I have postulated. Again, this breakdown is part of the business proposal and should be used to attract investors. Therefore, it should comport with reality and yet present an amount that is affordable. If the investment is too great an amount, potential partners may balk at the amount of money they are being asked to put in. The more you are requesting, the more vital it is to prove in the proposal that you have done your homework and can make good deals on all equipment.

Obviously, the cost will be greater if you include the billiard part of the business, and probably riskier as well, because the square footage of the room will need to be greater, which will only add to your bottom-line cost. I might add that people who play pool also drink and eat, and so if you can fill those pool tables with players it should pay off.

Putting these figures in a business proposal shows prospective partners that you have considered most or all of the expenses of opening and running this location. It also gives them a good idea of how much money will need to be raised to get your business off the ground.

## LOCATION

This section of the business proposal is again an explanation of how a location will eventually be viable and aid in the success of your operation. A prospective investor or backer may want to visit this location to better visualize what you are portraying in your business proposal.

Is a freeway close to your location? Is it in a busy shopping center? What are the demographics in the area as far as income per capita? Is it an area where people, particularly women, will feel safe in attending? The answer to these questions should all be positive; the reader should get a good feeling about the attractiveness of your location. The prospective investor might feel enthused, like you are, after reading the explanation of your location and visiting the actual space where you plan to put your dream business. Even if the investor isn't particularly excited about the business or the industry, he should feel confident in the potential of profits.

Most investors choose to place their money where they feel the returns are guaranteed, or at least as assured as can be. Give them that assurance through your business proposal.

In conclusion, in constructing your business proposal, remember that the exercise of formulating it for an investor's eyes will enable you to become clearer in your vision, in how your place will operate and the amount of actual business it will do.

Your business proposal should also inspire enthusiasm and self-motivation as you write down in detail how your business idea will operate in the real world, and the revenue it will produce for you.

# POS (POINT OF SALE) SYSTEM

**M**ost of us in retail have dealt with a cash register, ringing up a sale, making change, and handing it to the customer. Now, of course, everything is computerized and a good POS system is of paramount importance. They are all touch screens now, and will categorize and itemize items sold, and even compute a daily sales report, indicating how much is owed for cash and credit cards. The systems now will even compute your payroll. For these reasons, you need a quality POS system.

We opened in the beginning of 1994 with a POS system named Hospitality Systems Incorporated, or HSI. This POS system was efficient and enabled us to easily enter a myriad of items into the system. I wanted to see what beers were sold in a six-month period, all I needed to do was go into the program and type in "standard menu mix." I could then enter the dates that I wanted to analyze, and print out the types and amounts of beers sold in that period. This enabled me to get rid of beers that weren't selling well and sample new kinds. We now have a few revolving taps, but most beers have been on tap for years.

This is important for food as well. Seeing how many All-American Burgers are selling, for example, will allow you to understand which items to eliminate and which to promote. If you can see it is a good seller, then you can create a similar item and promote that item too. Our best sellers per category are appetizers. Every month or so I will go into the mainframe and pull up appetizers and see what has been hot during the past few months. Usually our wings are a best seller, and it is interesting to see how everything else relates to those sales.

Another important value of the POS is finding out how the same day did in sales last year. Say it's St. Patrick's Day and you want to see how much staff will be required for this year. Most systems will allow you to pull up the same day last year and get both a total sales figure for last year and a semblance of what the day will produce this year. It should even give you an hourly sales report.

Critical as well is the record for employees clocking in and out on your POS system. The time clock is built into the POS system, and will make a record for you and even calculate a large part of your payroll. We also use a payroll company to write final checks and take care of state and federal deductions. There needs to be a complete record of employees clocking in and out for every shift. I recently discovered that lunch breaks (especially in California) need to be recorded on your system because they are mandatory. There is no wiggle room here. All employees must take a 30-minute lunch break and cannot work off the clock in our state, period.

We recently wanted to upgrade the system that we had been using for 22 years, but we thought HSI was out of business. We went with a competitor and found this move to be a big mistake. The touch screen system was difficult for employees to navigate, and the records we received for history of sales and payroll were confusing and incomplete. After much wrangling with this company, we managed to get out of the contract we had with them, and fortunately found that HSI was still around but had a new name, 24/7. Now employees and management are happy again.

For billiard room owners, many pool table time systems are available. Some can even be incorporated into your POS system. For our pool tables, we continue to use a system we bought some 20 years ago as it still works well for us. We clock the rack out instead of the pool table, and the simple system we have works fine. Remember, if it ain't broke . . .

In short, since you will likely need a good POS system, research all models and find what works best for you. This will mean they will need to give you a demonstration and a sample of payroll and sales reports. Is the system employee-friendly for ringing in sales and managing payroll? Will it give complete, easy-to-read reports that you find beneficial and user friendly? A good POS system is a necessity for a business to operate at its highest capacity.

We carry 33 beers on tap, and draft beer is our highest profit center. The POS will indicate which draft beers have been selling best in the past few months, and allow you to replace those that are not selling. Also, it will show the mixed drinks and specific alcohol that are hot sellers and give an actual readout of all categories of sales.

The POS system is where technology can really help you streamline your business to maximize profits, instead of having to intuit what is selling the best. This is one of the most important purchases in opening your sports bar or billiard room.

# HIRING A BUILDING CONTRACTOR

It is of the utmost importance to check your funds and see how much you can realistically afford for a contractor to demo and build out your business. We knew up front that funds would be limited, and so we searched for someone who was readily available, reasonable cost-wise, and capable of doing this type of work. A tall order!

If you have plenty of capital to spend on a contractor who hires his own help and also uses an architect to deal with necessary agencies, then I would go that route, but oversee everything that is done. The contractor should know that funds are limited, and that you are paying attention to the amount they are spending. If he or she feels they have an open checkbook, it can really cost you in profits early on. This type of contractor will typically have an electrician, plumber, tile setter, drywall installer, etc., available. And they will have access to an architect. Remember, though, you will pay for this first-class service. Easier for you stress-wise, but you will pay for that convenience and comfort.

Another way to go would be to hire someone who is licensed and bonded, and has a small crew, but is a smaller company. They may have to outsource certain things, like architectural renderings, plumbing, or electrical. When jobs are outsourced to subcontractors, they usually come at a lower cost. Especially if you are supervising all jobs and keeping track of charges.

And then there is the way we did it. I knew that if we went with a licensed contractor, funds would probably run out at some time. We were strapped for cash, and needed to open as soon as possible.

Through my contacts in the bar industry, I met a man who had at one time built theater sets. He had also built a bar and done remodeling on several commercial establishments. He needed the work and money.

*Mike Lynch and Fred Rocha. They built most of Danny K's.*

Fred Rocha began the work of demolishing and building Danny K's in the summer of 1993. He was accompanied by an Englishman who was a little timid in doing demo work. After the first day, the Englishman was gone and Fred hired longtime friend and jack-of-all-trades Mike Lynch. This would be the duo that did 90 percent of the work at Danny K's.

Fred was able to work on a salary basis (per month). Mike was paid a decent hourly wage. During this time, a recession had hit the country hard, and most people needed the employment. We were grateful to get two qualified men, who needed work, to do most of the building of our business.

In a case such as this, where no one has a contractor's license, the owner of the business (myself) becomes the owner-builder. So I was responsible for contacting a possible electrician, tile setter, and drywall installer. We used subcontractors for everything else.

*Our bar almost ready to be painted.*

I approached the City of Orange, and they recommended a designer who lived in Orange to do architectural drawings. This designer was doing the work of an architect but did not have the same credentials, so he was cheaper. The city planning and building departments knew him personally, so he knew what they required with architectural renderings. He had a good personal relationship with the workers in these departments. This made it easier to get things approved.

I had sold my previous business, DK CUES, and had the money to stay on the job each and every day and monitor what everyone was doing. Fred was a full-fledged carpenter and knew what was needed for the construction. We would meet every morning, Monday through Friday, at 7:30 a.m., and together we'd decide what the agenda would be for that day.

They would begin working, and I would make a list of everything I needed to pick up, mostly at Home Depot. I still had my van that I used to sell cues for DK CUES, so I would bring back loads of drywall, plywood, hardware, paint, and anything needed for the day. After six months of this, I was not a happy shopper at Home Depot. Now it's a pleasure to go in there again.

*The game room was the babysitting room for those working out at the gym. A nice addition!*

Fred was, and still is, a very hard worker and does not waste his time. He and Mike were at it all day long and rebuilt Danny K's in about six months. Not bad, considering the amount of work they did. I would take the architectural renderings completed by the designer to the city and schedule inspections. Because I was on the job, dealing with the city and health department, the job ended up costing about half as much as it would have using a contracting company.

Looking back on it now, I can say with confidence that I would do the construction process the same way all over again, even if we were flush with cash. Being there every day as an owner-builder gives a better sense of everything that has been created in the place. It's like nurturing your wife when she's pregnant. It will be your child, and you will protect it.

*We used the existing upstairs floor for the bar soffit.*

It is of utmost importance to hire a contractor who will work with you to get exactly what you want and at a reasonable price. At the same time, you must always remember to get what you want, but at all times think about the cost. Your investors will appreciate that as well.

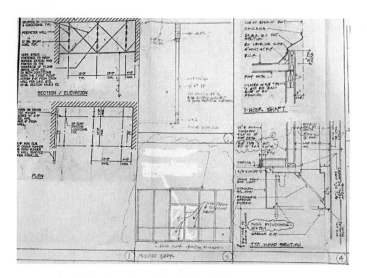

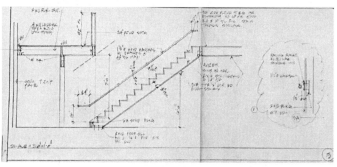

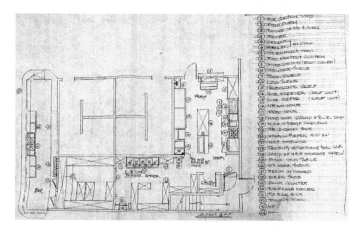

*Architectural drawings submitted to the city building department.*

# GETTING OPEN

Now that you have dealt with the local city regulations and the health department, you can begin building your dream sports bar and/or billiard room. Once the planning commission has signed off on your operation, building permits need to be pulled from the city building department. A health permit from the County Health Department will need to be pulled as well.

I used the architect's design to pull a "permit by owner" to build out Danny K's. The City of Orange inspected everything as we had it done. The walling in of the restrooms, the plumbing for the bar, restrooms, and kitchen—all of these were inspected before they were filled in and concreted over.

*Circa 1994. We opened with 20 taps, and added 13 more a year later. Note the 13" TVs.*

In our particular building, we had a mostly unfinished existing upstairs area that we wanted to use for an office and storage. Therefore, it needed to have its own architectural rendering. A stairway needed to be built, and the area had to comply with the city's code for fire sprinklers, electrical, etc. Even though this cost us more in money and time, it paid off nicely, because our offices and storage are still utilized upstairs.

It is necessary, of course, to pull a health permit. Sometimes the building permit from the city will overlap with the county health permit, but they usually won't contradict each other. They will demand that all of your cooking equipment fits compactly underneath the exhaust hood. The hood itself will need to meet certain requirements as well as the exhaust system (usually a water-cooled system).

Pay close attention to the restroom and kitchen requirements regarding walls and flooring. As I mentioned earlier in the book, we were forced to replace our flooring in the restrooms because the city required that it be a lighter color. This was my fault. I had so much going on at the time the flooring was installed that I had forgotten Health Department regulations. My bad.

The architect should be familiar with health department restrictions as well as what the building department requires. This is why it is important to hire an architect (or designer) who is familiar with these agencies' requirements.

The building inspectors will inspect every step of your remodel, so don't close up the plumbing until it has passed inspection. Because we had all of these pool tables and a very high ceiling, one building inspector demanded that we have four chains attached to each pool table lamp hanging from the ceiling. This was a pain and seemed inconsequential, but I can see the reasoning now. In case of an earthquake, they are more stable.

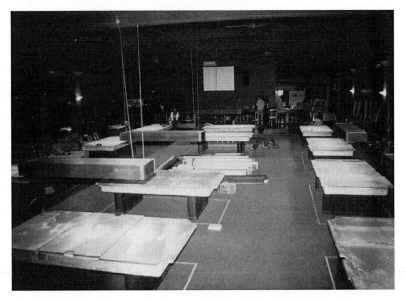

*We put tape on the floor to designate the pool table placement.*

We had a bonus room inside Danny K's to the side that was about 12 feet by 50 feet or so. When the space was a gym, that room had been used as a place for kids to wait for their parents while they were working out. We demolished part of the room, and made what remained into a game room that has a shuffleboard, foosball, and steel-tipped darts. We made nice arches opening into this room, and, of course, the size of the openings was inspected by the city.

*We had some lumber delivered, but I picked up most of everything we used at Home Depot.*

Complications arose from the size of the back room at Danny K's, threatening our getting open. It is about 6,000 square feet, and one of the building inspectors told me that the room was too big by itself for our occupancy allowance, which is 299 for the entire building. I explained to him that the room was going to contain 20 or so pool tables, and it would be unreasonable for a horde of people to be in there, since most of the people would be shooting pool.

It takes a certain amount of space around each pool table for people to play, so the area could never be that crowded. He was adamant, though, and told me that I needed to put in another door near the bar and separate the two rooms. This particular inspector was very rigid and followed the letter of the law. Sometimes you will need to deal with people like this, and I recommend continuing to be nice and doing what you can to comply.

I had a friend who had opened a poolroom near Encinitas, California, and I asked him if I could borrow his records, which showed how many people are on a pool table at one time. His records indicated that the average amount of people playing pool was two or three. To make a long story short, providing these records shed enough light on the situation that the city okayed the room and we were able to open.

The Design Review Board in the City of Orange also needed to approve our signage on the exterior sides of Danny K's. Typically every city will have restrictions and regulations on signage. We had awnings made with lighting behind them and carefully chose a color scheme and décor for the outside of the building. They okayed the colors we proposed for the exterior of Danny K's, and our landscaping.

The finishing touches of Danny K's took longer than I predicted, and it became frustrating for me because we needed to open to begin making money. Every day was a missed opportunity to make profits that would be used to pay back all this work being done over the course of six months. Those final weeks were the most pressured: painting walls, finishing the bar, staining counters, etc., all takes more time than you might think. These small finishing touches require time and attention because they are what the public will actually see when they enter your establishment. So don't rush. Dig into your stores of patience, and give yourself some time for these things to be finished properly.

I thought we were about ready to open, and I called the health department for a final inspection. I was informed that the lady working on our case had just left for a two-week vacation! We tried not to panic, and instead we used those two weeks to finish things up. We waited out the two weeks while remaining busy and using the time well. Things like this will happen. Don't let it pull you under. Just keep your head down and continue working.

One thing that was important before opening was training the bar and wait staff. During this extra two weeks before opening, we spent a lot of time training, teaching the staff our way of doing things and the POS system. It turns out those unexpected extra two weeks were really helpful in getting ready for opening.

In short, make sure you spend ample time with the agencies that will give final approval of your establishment. Ask questions, become informed, and try to follow the letter of their law.

*Opening night at Danny K's, January 28, 1994. Notice a*
*young Eddie Ortega. He still works for us.*

# DAILY OPERATIONS

Now that you are open for business and up and running, the task of operating the business and keeping it open is at hand. Paying attention to detail is very important now. Is everything in its right place? Is there a server's purse in view where it should not be? Is a box of glassware out in the open where customers can see it? I use the Disneyland example for how my place should look: everything should be in its rightful place and what the customers see should appear perfect.

Danny K's is like a large bar in a way.

We don't have a host or hostess who seats people. Our customers are welcome to come in and either check out a rack of pool balls or seat themselves. I have seen places my size that do seat people, and if that works for your place then that is fine. This is a matter of personal preference, I believe. In the beginning, we really could not afford to pay the extra person to seat people. Once we could afford to hire such a person, we decided it works fine for us this way, and we're not likely to change it now.

Once the customer has entered and sits down or begins a game of pool, they should be greeted right away by a server. If you've ever been to a bar and not been able to get a beer or drink within a couple of minutes, you may think twice about going back in. There are no excuses for not greeting guests right away and taking their order.

If they are ordering food, the kitchen should immediately start preparing the meal. Sometimes customers are there for lunch, and they may only have 30 minutes. In America we work countless hours per week, and we usually only have a limited amount of time for lunch. The cooks should know how to prep certain foods ahead of time to decrease the time it takes to get the food out. Customers can go to Del Taco and get food in minutes. Why would they come to your place if their wait time causes them to rush through lunch?

Sports bars and restaurants are in constant competition to draw customers to their establishment. Waiting time is a factor customers take seriously when choosing where to go. It's important to understand that everything needs to be delivered quickly. If you've been to restaurants or bars and watched employees talking with each other and not focusing on service, you can bet that this bar or restaurant will not be around for the long haul.

Now that your service is quick and efficient, your employee attitudes toward customers must be assessed and addressed. Is wait staff happy when they approach customers? Smiling? Or are they just going through the motions of doing the job?

We treat our employees the way we would like them to treat our customers. It's as simple as that. We are never angry with employees. Expectations are explained clearly with encouragement and with the understanding that the expectations are for the customers' best interest, which drives any change required. Any adjustments required by the wait staff are in their best interest, too, so instructions are presented in a good way. The atmosphere where employees spend much of their life should be one where they can be happy. If management is getting angry with employees, it effects the quality of their time at Danny K's, and is likely to transfer to their treatment of customers.

*Joyce has been with Danny K's for 21 years. Always a good attitude, and loved by all*

At the end of the day, workers can finish their shift with a smile, and not think about Danny K's any more. I only require that they are focused and do a good job while they are in my employ. After work or before is their time to use as they choose. This way they come in fresh and can offer friendly, good service again. This will ultimately have a positive effect on their private lives as well, and it can set a good standard for them if and when they leave my employment.

If your business can distinguish itself by offering a service that is a level above the competition, you will be amazed at the return business and the recruitment of regulars to your bar. Regulars make up a sizeable percentage of my clientele at Danny K's. I meet people all the time who have been coming in either since we opened or for 10 years or more. When the economy is bad, these regular customers will help you with overhead and staying afloat.

I recently went on a Mediterranean cruise that boarded in Spain. (I have been traveling a lot lately, trusting my GM and crew to run Danny K's). I decided to spend a couple of days in Barcelona and experience that seaside city.

I was sitting at a small bar that had a display of meats and fish, kind of like a deli, and drinking a glass of wine, when I was overcome by one of the strongest odors I had ever had experienced on this earth. I swiveled around on my stool and noticed this old couple, in their nineties probably, balancing themselves on canes, carrying their leftover bags of food and approaching the cash register, credit card in hand and now standing next to me.

The old man fumbled with his credit card, trying to insert it and swipe it, shaking all the while and finally was able to maneuver it into the slot. Meanwhile, the waitress had followed them out from the seating area, making sure that they were escorted in a friendly manner out of this place.

The smell was so overpowering I almost had to retreat to the restroom, just to save my olfactory senses. To say that they smelled like old people who hadn't taken a bath in months would be an understatement. Even the cook had emerged from the kitchen to waft his hand across his nose to underscore how awful this putridity was.

Finally and mercifully the man was able to complete his transaction, and they creaked and stumbled out of this deli, the waitress now visibly and involuntarily gagging in mid-air, trying not to lose her lunch. The smell lingered for a while, but they opened the front door and it receded and I figured I would live to see the late afternoon.

I spoke with the guy in charge about this, and why they would not try to rectify this situation with the old couple. Maybe hint to them that they could clean up a bit? I know it would have been awkward, but think of the other patrons there for lunch, who had to endure this sensory torture? He told me, like most restaurant owners, that the couple had been coming in for 40 plus years and he didn't want to offend them.

I said, in my limited Spanish vocabulary that I would have mentioned this to the couple. It may seem rude or insensitive, but remember the number one focus of any small business should be the customers' experience. The people adversely affected by the foul smell far outweighs the hurt feelings of two customers. When I think of this particular small restaurant, I can't help but associate my memory with this horrific odor. Sometimes it takes courage to state the obvious, and protect your source of livelihood. I believe anything can be said to someone, as long as it is said in a nice way.

By the way, I will always mention to the manager of a restaurant or bar my experience, good or bad. If it does not stand out at all, I will say nothing, but if the service and food are excellent I will always make sure the management knows. If my experience is poor, they will hear it also. I will not complain in any way, but I will inform them of my opinion, good or bad. I feel that if they hear this, it will help them do better, or reward the good service or preparation of food. And, I want to hear it at my restaurant.

How can you learn if no-one tells you or you hear nothing but compliments, even though the customer may have negative feedback? When I am in my place, I will ask customers, honestly about their experience, even if they don't know that I own the place. This way I will get an objective answer to my question. I will ask, "How are those wings", as if I am a customer wanting to order some for myself. I can handle the answer, and want to know, even if for some reason it is not exactly what I want to hear. This way I can make Danny K's a better place for a good experience. Employees need to somehow hear this negative feedback as well, but relayed by management in a positive way.

*Carol is our day manager and also tends bar. Everyone loves her.*

Of course, on occasion you will have employees who are having a bad day or are not in a good mood for whatever reason. Their personal life makes it difficult for them to be in the frame of mind to smile. They must leave their personal life at the door and be ready to act professional while on the job. There is no excuse to not smile and present a good attitude to customers. It is a basic requirement of delivering good customer service, which is what they are paid for and what they were hired to do. This should be part of the employee handbook. Stating this outright upon hiring, and highlighting it in writing in the employee handbook communicates that presenting a happy and pleasant front to the customers every day, without exception, is a prerequisite to working in your establishment.

*Eddie was hired before we opened. He is our longest working employee
at 24 years, and has a great demeanor and attitude.*

I have found many employees benefit personally from this
policy of exhibiting a positive attitude. Sometimes, after quitting to
move on to something else, ex-employees will come in and tell me
how much they got out of working in a place where they had to have
a good attitude. Cultivating a practice of presenting a positive attitude helps them personally in their lives beyond the doors of Danny
K's.

An attractive young lady worked for me for a couple of years,
and on occasion she would have a bad day and begin to complain to
other employees. I noticed the complaining, and pulled her aside to
let her know that no matter what type of day or week she was having,
her bad attitude ends when she enters Danny K's. She became more
jovial overall, and it not only helped her to get over her negative attitude at work, but I believed practicing a positive attitude even when
the mood was gloomy helped in her private life.

Communication with employees is somewhat an art, and
should always be conveyed as encouragement instead of criticism.

Instead of saying, "Don't do the job that way," you can suggest, "Here is a better way of doing this." And again, how you treat them is likely how they will then treat customers. This policy of a positive attitude goes for owners and management as well. When I am at Danny K's and an employee passes by me, I always smile. My GM does the same, with workers and customers. It creates an environment of positivity and happiness.

If a customer appears grumpy, I may approach him and ask, "How's it going today?' And sometimes he will say he had a tough day or whatever. By bringing it to their attention, I help those people see how they are acting, that their bad mood is shining through wordlessly. Simply asking a customer about their well-being goes a long way to lifting them out of a bad attitude. Someone noticed, and took the time to show he cared.

Since people will spend more time in a bar or pool room than in a restaurant, it's important that the clientele has a good attitude as well, because they can affect other customers. And because our employees have a good attitude, our customers do the same. My years studying the human psyche helped me to understand this important aspect of business.

# DEALING WITH CONTRACTORS AND PURVEYORS

Y ou will be dealing with an assortment of contractors after you open for business. Who will be your plumber? Your electrician? A/C maintenance company? Who will repair the bar equipment and furniture? A busy place is going to need ongoing repairs, with contractors and subcontractors maintaining equipment that is constantly in use. Think of these people as part of your business's team.

I found that in some cases, a smaller company with just a few employees will save you money and they can focus better on your needs. Larger companies often fail to offer good customer service. My electrician is a one-man operation, and can usually come out on a moment's notice to make any needed repairs. It is terrifying if the lights go out and the beer gets warm. If he is unavailable, then we can always call one of the larger companies that we have on file and get someone in to fix the problem as soon as possible.

My plumber is also very capable and has few employees. Again, a backed-up kitchen or restroom drain can really ruin your day and affect your profits. And this usually happens on a weekend when you are doing more business and is even more critical to have the repair done immediately. The plumber on my team is able to come at almost any time.

Also, I make sure that maintenance is done on the plumbing, because once a year or so the plumbing can back up from the main drain. I instruct the plumber to power jet out the main line once a year just for maintenance. This proactive approach will save you time, money, and stress on a busy night.

For air conditioning and cooling equipment, such as the walk-in coolers, food coolers, freezers, bar coolers, etc., I use a larger company that has a reputation for coming out right away and maintaining and repairing anything quickly and efficiently. They also come out every three months and change filters, and make sure that all units are in good working order. We have 35 tons of air conditioning at Danny K's, and at times, we need every bit of it. We use Trane air conditioners, which cost a little more than average A/C units, but last for years longer and very seldom break down. Our electrical bill is higher than most because we always keep the place cool. Worth it in the end, because customers enjoy the nice atmosphere.

If you have a large number of TVs, you will likely need a person who can fix any tech issues, for example, a receiver that no longer works, or a loose connection causing a fritz in the system. This person will usually be able to make any needed POS repairs as well. The POS maintenance is more important because it is critical to have the system working correctly to ring in and record sales. We do have receipt books just in case the system goes down. Here's where a Plan B is absolutely critical.

In 2007, lightning struck a pipe on the roof of Danny K's. It was early in the morning and the cleaning lady was working, when, Wham! The building shook and a small fire started in the upstairs storage area, where we have a lot of stereo and sound equipment. The pool tournament director found the poor janitor in the parking lot (she was in shock). He called the fire department, but the sprinkler system in the upstairs area put out the fire before they arrived.

I was scheduled to go on a road trip with my wife and daughter, and got a call at 8 a.m. that an emergency had taken place at Danny K's. I drove down and surveyed the damage.

There were some burnt wires, and minor fire damage to the upstairs area, but some electrical equipment needed to be replaced, and the sprinkler system kept releasing water. The entire back room and bar were flooded. I was not a happy camper, but sometimes acts of nature happen and all you can do is deal with it.

I thought of canceling my trip, but on second thought decided to let my general manager, Jami, take care of the issue. I figured this would be a good time for him to learn some of the trials I had gone through in building Danny K's in the beginning. He could call me with questions, and we could handle it by phone, and I could still go on my scheduled trip with my family.

Because we had all of these subcontractors in place, this arrangement worked fine. Our electrician Sal came down and replaced burnt wires and anything electrical that was damaged by either the fire or the water. My carpet cleaning crew sucked up all the water and cleaned and dried the carpet. A cleaning crew cleaned and dried the bar area. Jami contacted our sound and TV guy to come in and replace any damaged equipment. Our liability insurance agent was contacted, and we made a deal with the company to cover most of the repairs.

Without all of these subcontractors in place, this incident would have been a much more difficult job, and I would have needed to cancel my trip. But their names and phone numbers are on all managers' phone lists. Also, if one subcontractor is not available, there should be a back-up company to contact (a Plan B) so the repair can be done as soon as possible. Often times your main company may be busy on another job, or on vacation. I have phone numbers of several subcontractors in each area of expertise just in case the first in line on my team are busy.

In this situation with the lightning fire, we were closed for one day only. That's really quite remarkable when you consider the damage that was done. Since my place is large, we can work in one area and keep the rest of the business open.

Regarding contracting work, I suggest not using personal friends, because if something is not quite right with the final product, it is difficult to tell them that you are unsatisfied. A few years ago, I had 7,000 square feet of carpet replaced and went with a personal friend to do the job. My carpet installer noted that, after he laid it, the carpet was too thin for my type of operation. My friend initially disagreed, and this caused a small confrontation. We both had experts out to inspect the carpet, and in the end, we agreed that it was not adequate for my type of operation.

We had the carpet replaced, and all is fine now. But moving 20 pool tables back and forth to replace carpet is not fun. We had to do it twice. And the money I saved (originally) cost me more in the end. In short, get bids on everything major and avoid using services run by personal friends.

As I stated previously, we opened with an inadequate amount of electricity. Within a couple of years, I was able to add another 200-amp panel on a referral from another contractor. In this case, I saved thousands of dollars by using someone not from a major company but working for himself. Even though the man constantly complained about the work someone else had already done there, in the end we got our new panel and saved tons of money.

Using the right purveyors for your business is also very important. In some cases, like beer and alcohol distributors, you don't have much of a choice. Because you will need certain beers, such as Budweiser or Coors Light, only certain purveyors distribute them. But purchasing food is another situation.

As I stated before, we originally bought food from a company that turned out to be very expensive. So we researched wholesale food companies, and found that Sysco had the assortment of food we needed and the best prices overall. (Since then we are with Shamrock Foods. Same products but better prices.)

We purchase much of our produce from Restaurant Depot, because of the low price for the same quality you get from a renowned purveyor. It requires we pick up the food, but usually the expense of the time and drive is worth the savings. Food cost is always increasing, and wherever you can save money, it is important to do so.

You will probably need a linen company to deliver towels and aprons. We have been with the same company for years, and even though the prices have increased some, their service has been stellar.

With everything, keep a watch on volume. It is important to ensure no one delivers too much of anything, and therefore you pay for more than you need. Your kitchen manager should monitor what comes through the kitchen. If you are a small place and don't have a kitchen manager, monitor deliveries yourself.

We have a good pest control company as well. Keeping cockroaches out of the kitchen and bar is a must, of course. This company comes once a week, is reasonably priced, and they make sure that no insects infest Danny K's. Some things must be considered a fixed cost, and in my opinion, this is one of them.

We figure our own payroll, but we use a service to write the checks and calculate deductions on each check. Because we have a comparatively large payroll, it behooves us to use an outside company for this time-consuming task. Many smaller bars may prefer to do their own payroll, and this makes sense in many cases. We use PayChecks Payroll service, and they have proven to be reasonably priced and very efficient, with few problems. We used a larger company earlier on, whose name I will not mention here. Not only were they more expensive, we were constantly correcting mistakes that they were making. Saving money and better service is always a good deal.

We have our carpet cleaned once every six months. A small carpet-cleaning business gives us a great deal, and they also refinish the slate tile around the bar and dining area. Once again, keeping the place looking new and clean is a must in this business.

Kitchen hood cleaning is another cost that is critical to incur, because the health department will notice right away if the hood appears greasy. We allow the workers for the hood-cleaning company to come in at closing time, and ask that they exit by the time we open early in the morning. This is a service that should be done every four months or so.

In short, your contractors and purveyors are a necessary part of your business. They should be considered part of your team, and should be monitored constantly to make sure they are doing a good job for a reasonable price. In the end, we want to recognize a high net profit percentage, but not to the detriment of the overall function of the business. Spend wisely so that your services compliment your business.

# THE BUCK STOPS HERE

"The buck stops here" was first popularized by Harry S. Truman, who kept a sign with the phrase on his desk in the Oval Office. He believed that the President was responsible for the fate of the country, and would ultimately accept responsibility for all decisions made by any part of the government. I may not be running the country, but "The buck stops here" is a motto that I've come to believe is pertinent in any leadership role.

In fact, the responsibility of everything that happens in your establishment is yours. Therefore any mistakes ultimately fall on your shoulders. This is a wise way to handle the myriad of problems you will face in running a small business.

I first learned the value of this phrase in the early years at Danny K's. We had been open for three years or so, and I had hired a person to run security at the request of my partner. I was not wild about bringing John on, but as a favor to my partner I reluctantly agreed to hire him.

He was a smart person, but I wondered at the outset how dedicated to the business he would be. We trained him anyway at checking ID's and in the typical door host duties.

Of course a perfect storm hit when an agent for the ABC (Alcohol Beverage Control) happened to be inside of Danny K's, and an underage girl entered. Her ID was checked by John, and she was immediately allowed in, even though the front of the ID clearly read "Not 21 until (a date two years later)."

Since the bartender saw John check the ID, he assumed she was of age, and did not check her ID. She was served, and the ABC guy there jumped on it immediately. We were charged with serving an underage person. This can be a serious infraction and can result in the suspension of your license to sell alcohol. It can also mean jail time (eventually) for the server if there are multiple infractions.

So, I went for a meeting with the ABC person in charge to see what would be done about this infraction. We paid a fine of $3,000, a couple of grand for the attorney, and luckily were not given any points on our record. The person in charge at the ABC said, "I am a good judge of character, and I don't think you will do this again." He was right on both counts.

The bartender who served the young lady was also charged $3,000 and a grand for his attorney. He was put on probation for serving someone underage. All the bartender was doing was serving someone whom he had witnessed being carded by security. It is a very serious offense to serve someone underage in California. A bartender can even go to jail after a few offenses.

*Harry S. Truman believed that he should be responsible for things happening in government. A good philosophy to live by in business.,*

I was personally livid with this security guard. He had worked for me at a different business, and I knew he could be lax with people. I think he wanted to let the girl in, just to be a likeable guy. On top of all this, the security guard paid no fine, his only punishment was being let go by me.

I found myself resenting him for his actions, and my partner for convincing me to hire him. I wondered how someone could be so stupid as to jeopardize my business and cost us thousands of dollars in the process. Especially because she didn't even use a fake ID.

I was angry for quite a while before realizing it was truly my fault. My fault because I agreed to put my partner's wishes ahead of the best interests of Danny K's. My fault for not listening to my gut about John. And this was the lesson for me: I am the owner and operator of this business. All decisions end with me, and I am responsible for everything that happens here.

Amazingly, when I took responsibility for this action, I stopped resenting John and my partner. And I can guarantee that I never made a dumb decision like that again. I was taught many years ago that if I resent someone over a period of time, I don't really want them to change. I had to figure out what was driving the resentment, and make the change there. And forgiveness is a big thing, even in business.

By realizing that you are responsible for everything that happens in your business, the anger you feel towards others for making mistakes eases. You hired them, after all. I try to give everyone I deal with the benefit of the doubt, because I know most people's intentions are good, and they are usually trying their best. Sometimes, if their best is not good enough for your business, it is important to let them go, and hire someone else.

Recently I had some pool tables recovered, and decided to try someone other than my regular go-to guy, because I wanted the pocket openings changed, making the tables more to professional code. This would satisfy the more critical players in my room. I paid twice as much and realized after the job was finished that this man was worse—much worse—than Javier, who had recovered my tables for 20 years.

I had the new guy come back in and try to fix his bad work on the tables. The problem was that he was incapable of doing the job right. No matter how much time he spent on recovering and on the pockets, the tables were no better.

So I ate crow and admitted to Javier that I tried someone else and it didn't work out. He was okay about it and redid the bad work, and everything is good again. Forgiveness is important, and it goes both ways if you stay in business long enough.

I could have tried to get a refund from the new guy for some of the work done, and I could have resented and complained to others about him. I took responsibility and learned from the experience. I will use my regular go-to guy from now on. I know that the man who recovered my tables the wrong way was doing his best. I gave him the benefit of the doubt, but realized that he was not up to the task. I do not resent him, but will never use him again.

I have also experienced a few lawsuits at Danny K's that have cost us quite a bit of money. We are in California, and it is important to stay on top of legislation in this regulated state. So, whenever I am sued, I chalk it up to my lack of knowledge of recent state legislation, I try to settle, and then I move on. This is one reason I belong to the California Restaurant Association. The CRA gives updates on recent legislation and offers warnings to bars and restaurants of recent laws and rulings that can adversely affect business.

Ultimately all things that happen in your business will be your responsibility. When you realize this, and stop resenting those who have made the business more difficult, it will give you more spiritual and emotional freedom. And remember, "The buck stops here!"

# THE KITCHEN

When I opened Danny K's, we had a cook brought in from a popular restaurant chain in Orange County. He was able to make the plates that the GM and I had created to look and taste good. In the beginning, I had a series of firings, one of which was this head cook. After his exit, I had to train the series of replacements from that point on.

The head cook can train all of the dishwashers and prep cooks. My job as an owner and operator (back then) was to sample the food and ask customers what they thought about it. If I got negative feedback, I would speak with the head cook and make a constructive suggestion about what corrections to make. I found that getting angry at anyone on the job is futile and will only create bad feelings, which is never good for business. Most employees sincerely want to do well, and will listen to constructive criticism. If you appeal to their good side, you will get their best.

One problem I had with a cook I had promoted to head of the kitchen after another cook quit, was that he could not speak English. Even though he was a good cook, I could not speak enough Spanish to fully communicate with him. He also had a difficult time communicating with servers.

On one busy lunch, he didn't understand me when I told him that we needed to prep a full broiler of chicken breasts. He would always nod like he knew what I was saying. Needless to say, the lunch was a disaster because he had not prepped enough chicken breasts.

And so I promoted another cook who could communicate with me. Open communications with all employees is extremely important. The kitchen equipment needs to be of high quality, even if it is used. Used equipment will work for many operators who are slightly underfunded (like I was). You can expect that on occasion a piece of kitchen equipment will break or stop working at any time. Coolers or freezers that are operating to their limits in the height of summer will at times shut down on a Saturday night, when you are at your busiest and cannot call anyone in to fix them. For this reason, it is imperative to have high-quality, efficient coolers and freezers. A breakdown during a busy time can be very frustrating. Having a good air conditioning company to keep the equipment maintained is so important.

What would you like your menu to consist of? Since Danny K's is a very eclectic business and we cater to a wide array of people who are watching sports, playing pool, or just hanging out in a bar, our menu is large and diverse. Customers will stay at Danny K's for one to five hours or so, and sometimes eat two meals in one visit here. This is why we offer a menu that has everything from large salads, sandwiches, appetizers, pizza and pasta, tacos, steaks, and ribs—with several variations of each.

Your menu should reflect the theme and atmosphere of your establishment, and the clientele who will spend time there. For instance, you might not want to have only Mexican food on your menu if you have a diverse clientele. Having a Mexican food dish or two on the menu is a good idea though, especially in Southern California. If your kitchen is really small with no exhaust hood, you can make salads and serve meat and cheese plates, or microwave sandwiches. Determining whether your menu will offer a range of foods or focus on one particular cuisine should be determined by the nature of the business and the clientele base.

The local health department will inspect your kitchen once every three months or so, and cleanliness is imperative. In some counties in California, kitchens are given letter grades, and in those areas it is important to have an A rating. In areas that give a pass/ fail, a pass is mandatory, because the kitchen can be shut down with a fail notice. The kitchen head and management need to work with the health department and keep every aspect of the kitchen clean. It's not necessarily a pleasant job to keep the kitchen spotless, but if you consider you are serving food to the public, you can understand why it must be this way.

*Marco, our kitchen head started as a dishwasher and has been with us for 15 years. Maria, in the background has been with us for 20 years.*

Even though our kitchen is small, we're able to prepare a wide variety of food. One reason we are able to make all these different dishes is that we have similar ingredients that we can put into many of the entrees. For instance, we use chicken breast for salads, sandwiches, pizza topping, appetizers, and taco meat. Ground beef is used the same way, but for hamburgers, taco meat, and pizza topping. This way you're not purchasing so many different products that it requires lots of storage space. Also, the more kinds of food you have, the more likely they can go bad. When creating your menu, take note of this. Preparing a wide range of food with a limited amount of ingredients helps to keep your costs down.

For the kitchen helpers and employees, like other areas of employment in your establishment, keep an eye on the payroll! I've seen businesses where there are so many employees standing around that you know this is cutting deeply into the net profit. Danny K's has had to work on a very lean budget since opening, and so we try to keep the number of employees working on a shift at a minimum. This also works well for servers and bartenders, because their tips will be higher, and thus happier working in your place. It also keeps everyone working and feeling more productive than if people are idle with nothing to do.

The kitchen is one of the cylinders of your engine that needs to be focused on all of the time you are open, and even before the doors open for business. The prep work should be carefully thought out, with as little waste as possible, in order to maximize your net profit. To make the kitchen profitable, give it the attention it deserves—the kitchen is a major part of your business.

# MANAGING EMPLOYEES

There is an art to training and managing the people you hire. They should represent your intended theme and approach to doing business. Every person on your staff is an extension of your business. If it appears that they don't care, whose fault is it? Management. Everything that happens is due to either my goodwill or a mistake that I have made. Taking responsibility for employees' behavior is important. Accepting responsibility for the people on my staff means I am the one who will make the change happen if adjustments must be made, one way or another.

How do we ensure that employees are always smiling with a good attitude? During training, we let them know what we expect when they wait on customers. Even though attitude is number one with us, it is still important to stress other parts of the job, like bussing tables, side work duties, learning the POS system, and making sure that customers do not walk out on tabs.

We may be somewhat different than some sports bars in that we require a credit card be given to the server before drinks or food is delivered. Most restaurants do not require this. Because we are a restaurant and bar, patrons will sometimes stay for many hours and will at times forget to pay. With regular customers, this is not always an issue, because they will pay the next time they come in. But many customers are from out of state, or on a business trip, and will only visit Danny K's once a year or so. For most customers, we require a credit card as a deposit. I'm not particularly fond of this procedure, but it ensures that we are paid for what we have sold. In the early days of opening Danny K's, we needed every penny to stay in business, so we have continued the process because there are no questions about walk-outs.

The side jobs, which consist of refilling ketchup bottles, salt and pepper shakers, parmesan cheese dispensers, cleaning the wait station (or bar), etc., need to be done every day by every employee. During employee meetings, these issues are discussed. Those who are not doing their job will be told and expected to make the correct adjustment.

We have three scheduled employee meetings per year, and require all servers to attend. Even though these meetings are inconvenient for almost everyone, the results pay off on the floor. We stress customer service as a number one priority in these meetings, which means getting to all customers on a consistent basis, and with a good, happy attitude. We have an outside patio, and for some reason servers tend to forget to go out there. So, in employee meetings we walk the floor and let everyone know where they need to go for the best possible service.

Also in meetings, we encourage open dialogue about items that employees wish to address, such as other servers not doing their job, etc. Only positive and encouraging comments are welcome. This way the employees can express their opinions, but in a positive way so there are no hard feelings between employees and/or management. If a meeting turns into a bitch session, and people openly criticize the system or fellow workers, usually problems will not be resolved. I have found that someone who complains about a situation usually does not want it resolved. So, constructive criticism is always welcome, and will generally be met with positive results.

Our meetings are held on weekends, because many servers work other daytime jobs. Weekend mornings, usually Sundays, are the best for us. Of course, many servers have worked the night before and are tired at nine a.m. on Sunday morning. We are always lax and offer donuts and coffee. But the meetings are mandatory, and very important. New employees can better understand company policies and intentions of management when they attend these meetings. I have noticed that in this business, some things are not the most convenient and require uncomfortable, difficult work. But if you want to be a success, these tasks need to be scheduled and done.

Some restaurants number their tables for servers to enter into the POS to indicate the party they are waiting on. We do it a bit differently. Servers are assigned areas of the room, and tables that are diagramed on the POS screen are highlighted when a tab is opened. Since we are a combination bar and restaurant, customers tend to move around from one area to another. For this reason, we do not number the tables, only the party.

Our best servers are the ones who can work reasonably fast, with few mistakes and maintain a good, happy attitude. There is never an excuse to be unhappy at Danny K's. In the case of any issues between employees, we encourage some form of open dialogue. My general manager Jami Jun and I are always open to hear any problems employees may have with one another or with management. This includes any type of sexual harassment an employee may perceive, such as unwanted advances or remarks from someone in the workplace. The employee meetings confirm that we are there to hear whatever is on their minds.

Of course, I need to emphasize how important it is to have enough employees on a busy night. Without enough employees, not only will you develop a bad reputation for not giving good service, but your sales will also be compromised. In this age of social media, you can immediately either get a good or bad review on Yelp or

Google, and people actually do read these reviews. We want four or five star reviews.

Having the right amount of people on the floor is a constant give and take, a constant calculation finding an accurate estimate of what you need at a given time. Too many employees on the clock will cost the business in net profit, and too few will also cost in net profit, because of lack of sales and the possibility of creating a bad reputation. It is truly something to study and take seriously in your business.

As with servers and bartenders, the head cook, prep cooks and dishwashers, all must receive mandated lunch breaks. Even if they request no lunch breaks, the State of California mandates a lunch break where they clock out and then back in. Other states may have different rules, but if you can follow the more strict rules from the beginning, it will be easier to follow them when the state mandates more rigid laws.

I have learned the hard way to "give to Caesar what is Caesar's." This is a quote from Jesus Christ when a citizen asked about paying taxes. And it is appropriate here, because even though the state may not always seem fair, it is the law. The sooner you can get used to obeying all the laws, regardless of whether or not you agree with them, the more routine they become.

# HANDLING EMPLOYEES
## (AS OPPOSED TO MANAGING)

How you deal with employees is a major part of any operation of a decent size. Danny K's employs 35 managers, bartenders, servers, cooks, and security personnel. All employees work together to make sure that Danny K's operates like a well-oiled machine. Because most employees are in the public eye, it is necessary for them to portray an attitude of friendliness and happiness, so attitude needs to be high on the list when interviewing employees.

The ability to do the job, of course, goes without saying. Servers need to learn the POS system quickly and work at a fast pace. Bartenders need to work fast, responsibly, and efficiently, and do so with a smile and good attitude. And their relationship with all employees should be direct, friendly, and encouraging.

Management is always concerned about the operation—yet needs to be direct, supportive, and encouraging to all employees. Criticizing employees or acting upset with their job performance will only create resentment and alienation within the work force. When I let go of three managers to save money and took charge of managing employees, it took me a while to understand that getting angry with them over jobs done incorrectly was only creating internal resentment and group anxiety towards me and others in charge.

I learned after a year or so that it is much more productive to point out a flaw and then encourage the right or better way to do the job. This is not the army, and we are not drill sergeants. And they are not enlisted troops. Many of my employees are single moms or dads and are working many hours in a week to provide for their families.

And since they spend much of their lives working at Danny K's, I prefer making their experience here a good one. There is never a reason to be upset with an employee, and if I am ever upset or angry, I will wait a while and come back to apologize for my behavior. All of us have a tendency to want to blame someone for a mistake that can hurt the business. Some may think that blowing off steam by taking out frustration on the person who made the mistake is a solution, but I know it creates more, and larger, problems.

Several years ago, after the recession of 2008, my CPA sent an amount of taxes to be paid to my in-house bookkeeper. My bookkeeper called me and said that it was a lot of money. I responded, "It's always a lot of money." And so I didn't ask the amount and told her to just pay it. It turned out to be about $20,000 more than our normal tax contribution. And so we now had taken an extra $20,000 out of our account and paid it to the IRS. There was no way of getting this money returned. We had to take it off of our next tax-estimated payment. This was a lot of money to be extracted from our account unexpectedly. And with the economy taking a turn for the worse, we could not earn enough income to cover it. So I had to convince my wife (at the time) to take $10,000 out of our personal account and put it into the business account. She laid the responsibility at my feet for the error, and I tried to explain that several people (not just me) had made mistakes and that it would eventually be rectified.

I was tempted to get angry with my CPA for giving my bookkeeper the wrong information. I was also tempted to become upset with my bookkeeper for not telling me exactly what the tax burden was. In actuality, I was the one who had not asked for the information. I knew better than to become upset and so I remained calm, not looking to blame anyone for the mistake but accepting full responsibility. And even though this put a further strain on my marriage, I was able to avoid alienating any employees or outside help over a simple mistake. Learning to stay calm with employees is an invaluable asset. They will trust you and your disposition, and you will get more out of them when you remain calm. Remember to encourage, not criticize.

Most people grow up with plenty of criticism from parents, siblings, and relatives. Why should they work an eight-hour day with criticism that will affect their work and make their day miserable? I teach all managers at Danny K's to encourage and never be angry when dealing with employees. There is always constructive advice to give an employee who has done something against company policy. You can say, "This is what I would recommend for the future," or "Maybe if you did it this way. . ."

When I was 18 years old and driving an ice cream truck on the Fort Huachuca Military base in Arizona, I sometimes had issues with cleanliness of the inside of the ice bin, which used dry ice to keep the ice cream frozen. The owner rode with me to the base one day and suggested, "You seem to do a very good job selling the candy and ice cream, and we really appreciate that; but I think you could improve by being a little more tidy?" This worked for me, and I began to clean better. I never forgot how he gave me constructive criticism, and how it made me feel. It's a model for how we work at Danny K's.

Of course, if the mistake is a severe violation of company policy, the person will need to be written up and warned that continued violations may lead to dismissal. But even this can be done without anger. I usually let the employee know after a write-up that as far as I am concerned this never has to happen again, and I expect they will learn from the mistake.

Under most state laws, an employee must be written up at least three times before they are let go. This will guard against any lawsuits brought forth by the employee and will also ensure that they will not be able to file for unemployment insurance. I know this may sound harsh on my part, but unemployment insurance can skyrocket if you are not careful. Also, a server can usually find a job within a few days, and so it is not a necessity for them to go on unemployment. In a good economy, jobs in this industry, as a general rule are plentiful.

Employees are one of a service businesses' greatest assets. They deal with the other most important asset of a business, the customers. Yes, these are the two critical assets a business such as mine has—employees and patrons. Remember, how you treat your employees is how they will treat the public. If you want them to be helpful, friendly, and conscientious, act accordingly to them. They represent you, and your business, to the customer.

# THE BAR

This is where the heart of an operation like mine exists. If my general manager is not present or if I'm not there, the head bartender is in charge of Danny K's. He or she will make major decisions like cutting employees when it becomes slow and calling in someone to clean up a mess in the restroom. I was the only manager at Danny K's for a long time except for whoever was in charge of the bar. This puts more responsibility on the bartender in charge, but it teaches them management skills and how to make crucial decisions. Joyce Miller and Eddie Ortega have been with Danny K's for a combined 43 years, and both know what we expect and how to handle crises.

The bar is also the heart of the operation because the most profitable items are sold there. We sell more draft beer than anything else, with liquor being a close second. Our draft beer cost is 23 percent, and we sell considerably more draft than any other product at Danny K's. Liquor is a distant second, but at a cost of 18 percent, it is highly profitable. The bar also makes drinks for all customers who enter, and since we have a 10,000-square-foot operation, the bartenders are very busy.

Our POS system is also housed at the bar. When a POS terminal on the floor needs some form of correction, it is usually done at the main bar terminal.

The bartenders need to always be happy and helpful. Customers usually see and meet the bartender first and then sit down to eat and drink or play a game of pool. Their personalities and attitudes are vital to the atmosphere and ambience of your business. Consistently good, quick service with a smile and a happy attitude is a way of ensuring that your customer will stay for a while and visit again. If a bartender does not exhibit this type of character, maybe they are in the wrong kind of profession.

*Right before we opened early in 1994. I worked behind the bar on occasion.*

Special attention must be given to the customers at the bar at all times. If a customer is eating a meal and drinking a beer, the bartender should offer a glass of water as a courtesy to go along with the food. I have been in many places where I have called out to the bartender for their attention because they are not noticing their customers at the bar. If you want to keep clients coming back to your bar, pay special attention to their needs. It will pay off in spades.

I have walked into many bars where the customers seem like afterthoughts, not as important as doing another task or speaking with another employee. A recent visit to a bar in Fullerton was particularly eye opening. I came in and sat at the bar, no one spoke to me for a few minutes, and then a waiter came up and said, "A bartender will be out here shortly."

I waited, and waited. I saw several employees milling about, but no one could pour me a beer? So they went searching for the bartender, and the waiter said, "He's doing something important back there, just not sure what it is."

I said, "Okay, I'll wait for another minute or so. If he doesn't show by then, I will need to go." A couple of minutes later, I took off.

Whatever pulled the bartender away from the bar may have been important, but the fact is that customer service needs to supersede everything else in the business. If something else is put before the customer, the business will suffer. Personal relationships, odd jobs, speaking with other employees, even business-related concerns, all need to take a back seat to the most important part of any business—the customer.

*A recent photo of the lighted bar and TVs. It is always kept neat and clean.*

A few months prior to this experience, I was in a barbecue place in downtown Fullerton, and had walked in for a beer and food. It took me a while to be waited on, and so when I ordered a beer I gave him a heads up and told the bartender that I would order food in a few minutes. Several people were at the bar and were served. That would be my last communication with the bartender for about 15 minutes. He seemed to be involved in a discussion with a female employee, and disregarded the bar for at least 10 minutes. So, I paid, walked up to him, and said, "I was going to order some food and stay for a while, but you never came back to ask me if I wanted something."

He seemed a little shocked, and said something like, "Oh, I am sorry, sir. I can help you if you like."

I said no, that he wasn't paying attention to anyone at the bar and I was no longer hungry for the barbecue.

I will not likely go into this establishment again. I am used to giving good customer service and I expect it in return. Your bartender acts as an ambassador for your place, so choose wisely. Who will be representing your business?

Many bars I have gone into have a sticky bar top, or fruit flies everywhere. And usually the bartender is standing there, idly waiting for a customer to order. If a spilt beer or coke has not been cleaned properly off the bar, then the incoming customer will face this mess. This is not the first impression to leave on your new potential patron.

*Mike Powers with his brother Chris, Mikey always donated to any of our causes and was extremely generous with employees and other patrons.*

The cleanliness of the bar is of paramount importance, and should be worked on continually when bartenders are not busy serving drinks or dealing with customers. Fruit flies can be a problem at most bars. An unclean back bar and bar top can pose a real problem to customers waiting for a drink. Sometimes sugars build up around the soda and juice taps, and these spigots need to be cleaned on a regular basis. When it is slow, the bartender can pull out wine bottles and clean behind them, empty out the coolers, and clean underneath the bar. It's not necessarily the most pleasant job, but it needs to be done consistently. Any bartender's purse or backpack should be hidden from view as well. Employees can sometimes, without thinking, leave a newspaper on the bar or something that appears out of place, and this clutter can appear unseemly. This is where the Disneyland effect comes into play again—everything should be spotless, in place, and never appear messy or cluttered or less than perfect. Like Disneyland, customers attend my business for the atmosphere and experience. Any dirt or clutter will detract from this effect.

For the bar owner and general manager, there are some definite "do's and don'ts" we all should follow at the bar. An old saying states (pardon my crudeness): "You don't shit where you eat." For instance, dating an employee is a definite don't. It compromises your position of authority and diminishes respect among other employees. And, if someday you should need to fire this person, they can come back and say that it was retribution for a relationship turned sour.

Talking politics, race, or religion is not a good idea either. These are usually hot topics that will alienate your employees and often times customers (your two greatest assets). On occasion, I will discuss politics with someone who is like-minded or who I know I will not offend during the discussion. If customers can discuss politics in a civil manner, we will not intervene. Only if they become loud and the conversation becomes heated will we step in to direct the attitude to our business's preferred ambience of relaxed comfort.

Drinking at your own bar is maybe a matter of personal preference. Many customers enjoy drinking some with the owner or manager, and in the beginning of opening Danny K's, I did drink to nurture friendships and patronage. I don't believe it to be a negative unless it injures your health or you become overly drunk. Socializing with customers is important, I do believe, even if you don't drink. Patrons enjoy getting to know the owner, and it can be a reason they become a regular.

It takes a special personality to be a good bartender. Some customers can be very difficult, even when they are not drunk. The good bartenders I have can easily let rude customers' attitudes wash over them like water off a duck's back. These people will not affect their mood for the day. A bartender taking things personally will soon become tainted and should not be in the industry.

Running a good bar like mine takes time and focus, as does all areas that are of crucial importance. It is one of the eight cylinders of the well-tuned engine that needs to be honed and improved in order to keep the smooth-running operation on track.

# CLICKING ON ALL
# EIGHT CYLINDERS

I liken the optimal functioning of a business to "clicking on all eight cylinders." All aspects of your business should run as well as possible. The following are what I would define as Danny K's eight most important cylinders:

*1. Service*

Service needs to be monitored at all times. It is an ongoing process to make sure that your service is the best in the area. I am always watchful that employees are smiling and happy when dealing with customers, making sure that they are attentive and offering good customer service.

*2. Employees*

Employees need to be treated with utmost respect and dignity. They are your representatives to your most important commodity, your customers. And they will be much more loyal to you if they are treated right. Never become angry with an employee. They will not represent your place in positive ways if you do. They will reflect the attitude that you convey to clientele.

*3. Management*

My general manager, Jami, is mindful of all aspects of these eight cylinders. And of keeping the place clean and in repair. My day manager, Carol, is also very much on top of things. We all work as a team to make sure that Danny K's is running like a fine-tuned machine.

## 4. Food

Even though food is not the major moneymaker for this business, food is a draw for a lot of customers and so meals need to come out looking and tasting good. We are always tasting the food and making sure that the products we purchase are of the very finest quality. This augments the rest of our business and creates happy customers.. The kitchen should always be clean and the cooks happy.

## 5. Bar

If you open a sports bar, tavern, or poolroom with a bar, the bar is where you make the lion's share of your net profit. The bar always needs to be clean and tidy, because customers are sitting right in front of the bar and looking directly at the back bar and will notice if they are dirty or in disarray. If you run out of a beer on tap or a particular bottle of alcohol, replace it as soon as possible. There is no excuse for a tap handle to produce no beer. Attention needs to be paid to the net profit here, because this is where most of your business is likely to be done. Waste and any type of pilferage needs to be monitored. Bartenders are fun and conscientious. Joyce, Eddie, and Carol have been with me for a total of 60 years, and represent Danny K's well.

## 6. Back of the House

Where you count your money, do the daily sales report, create flyers, make the work schedule, figure out payroll, and all other necessary behind-the-scenes functions is extremely important. Carol, Jami, and I are constantly up in our office coming up with different ideas of how to promote Danny K's.

## 7. Sports

If you decide to open a sports bar, it needs to be done right. We have all the subscriptions for NHL, MLB, NBA, NFL, UFC, PGA, most of soccer, and we focus on the customers' needs in terms of sports coverage on TV. Yes, they are needs. When a person gets off work and wants to watch their own game (that they can usually watch at home), it needs to be turned on for them, and right away. All of our TVs are clear and updated, and we have a reputation for having just about everything a person wants to watch. And we have a reputation for getting the game on right away. We have shown boxing telecasts ever since we opened, and we now have developed a reputation for having all of the fights, including UFC. We are considered number one in Orange County for places to go to watch fight telecasts.

### 8. Billiards

If you have pool tables, I recommend keeping them recovered and leveled at all times, as best as possible. Customers really do appreciate a level table with cloth that is not too faded. They will pay you back with continued patronage to your establishment. Also, keep the cue tips new and replenish your supply of pool cues. A triangle and bridge stick should always be at each table as well. Fernando Rivas is our tournament director and not only knows pool but also understands how to deal with people. He is a good representative for Danny K's and upholds our reputation well. As I said before, our pool tournaments have the highest participation in the nation, possibly in the world.

# SERVING INTOXICATED CUSTOMERS

I have made this topic into a chapter all its own because of the responsibility we as bar owners have in maintaining a healthy clientele by not serving them when they are visibly intoxicated. If my business sends an inebriated person out onto the local roads and freeways, what happens to this person becomes my responsibility.

By law in California, a business is no longer considered liable for over-serving someone who subsequently receives a DUI. This makes sense, because oftentimes a person will have something to drink after they leave your place, either in the car or from another bar. Even though you are not legally responsible as a bar owner for what happens after an inebriated patron gets behind the wheel, it is still (in my opinion) a personal responsibility we as bar owners should accept to make sure that patrons do not harm themselves or others.

We encourage servers to pay close attention to all drinking customers and make sure that they are not slurring their words or staggering while walking. When one of my staff notices someone who is obviously drunk, we will politely suggest something like, "Maybe you'd like some water now instead of alcohol?" A statement like this will usually make the customer aware of how much has been consumed. Or, we can offer the customers some chips and salsa and respectfully ask that they not drink for a while. If they become obstinate, then a manager needs to come over and let them know directly, "I'm sorry, but you've had too much to drink for now." And then if they become difficult, you can threaten to call the police. On occasion, we have had to follow through on that.

Since many of our customers become regulars and come in several times a week, we feel it is important to take care of them and make sure that they do not incur any difficulties from drinking at Danny K's. A DUI will cost thousands of dollars, a revoked driver's license for several months, and will stay on one's record for at least eight years. This becomes a big responsibility for us.

Intoxicated customers can also become loud and rude toward other patrons, so it behooves us to limit alcohol intake and make sure that patrons do not overconsume and disturb other customers. This is how you can create a good atmosphere, by making sure no one is too drunk or out of control. We have a few customers we will not serve hard alcohol to, because they become loud and raucous when they have even one drink. We respectfully tell these few patrons that we won't serve those kinds of drinks to them because of past experiences. They may not particularly like this rule, but sometimes it is a necessity for the overall benefit to them and other customers that they not become that drunk. This costs us money at times, but the overall effect on Danny K's is a major benefit, and it's the right thing to do.

Many bars will serve someone as long as they can stand, and not cut them off because they don't want to start a conflict or lose a profit. Confronting a customer in a nice way works to everyone's benefit. You help the person drinking too much as well as patrons who happen to be around this person by respectfully cutting them off.

Just because someone comes in and spends a lot of money does not make it right to allow them to alienate other customers and make them uncomfortable. This is where the term dive bar comes in to play. Dive bars are born when management allows the poor treatment of customers to continue. This is another way of looking at the big picture of your operation. Sacrificing a few dollars made from a few drinks for an overall atmosphere that customers appreciate is definitely worth the trouble. This will reflect in reviews on social media and through the word of mouth recommendations from happy customers.

# THE BILLIARD ROOM

The pool tables in your place need to be as good as you can possibly afford. I've found that if the tables are good, maintained, and recovered every year, customers will respond with making your place their regular hangout. I opened with 24 professional-size pool tables that I had custom made by a small manufacturer in Los Angeles. They are solid and heavy, with a diamond wood top rail. After 25 years, they still look great. If a scratch occurs on the top rail, it can be easily rubbed out with sandpaper.

Diamond pool tables are the standard in the industry, and they have diamond wood on the top rails like mine. They are well-known tables, and many professional events are now played on Diamonds. If you can procure some used Diamonds, I would suggest using them to open. Pool tables will last for 75 to 100 years, so it is not necessary to open with new tables. Older Gold Crown Brunswick tables are heavy, stable, and known for how well they play. The newer Brunswick Gold Crowns are lighter in weight and more cheaply made (in my opinion). Gold Crown 1's and 2's are the better tables.

*A view of our main pool area from the elevated stage. We began adding TVs when the popularity of pool began to wane.*

The space between the pool tables should be, on average, about 54 inches. A player then can shoot from the tip of the cushion and not be sitting on the adjacent table. Any closer and the players will feel cramped and uncomfortable when they are shooting one of these rail shots. From the wall, the tables need to be five feet away at a minimum. So if a ball is on the cushion and the player is stroking perpendicular to the wall, he or she will not hit the wall. A pool cue is typically 58 inches long, and so 60 inches away from the wall is an ideal distance. Any nearby pub tables or bar rails should not be a problem, because the players will stroke over them.

It is always a good idea to use professional-grade equipment. We use Brunswick Centennial balls and Simonis billiard cloth for the pool tables because many discriminating pool players frequent my place. Both avid and casual players benefit from this quality equipment. A lady recently reported on Yelp that "Danny K's has new pool tables." Not really. We just keep the tables recovered and looking nice. We also buy expensive house cues with pro tapers on the shafts. This means that the shaft diameter stays the same for 18 inches or so, and then tapers normally. This ensures that the stroke is nice for the players, and is not an encumbrance on the bridge hand. Customers recognize these amenities, even though they may not always talk to you about it.

There needs to be a seating area for each and every pool table. And in some places, we have several sitting areas for one table. This way, groups of people can play, gather around, and have a party while they are playing. Remember, the pool table time is a very small percentage of the overall profit your business will earn. Mostly the income will come from beer, alcohol, and food. So when these clients are shooting pool and having a party, they are consuming the life's blood of your operation. Areas for parties are very important, and keeping the pool tables nice encourages these people to want to shoot pool and be social while doing it.

*Stacey Novack, A pro who has come in to Danny K's since we opened. A nice person and a great player!*

At Danny K's we have the most successful weekly pool tournaments in the nation. I'm not suggesting that your poolroom do the same, but it's proved profitable for us. We have five pool tournaments a week, and draw between 16 and 40 players for each tournament. We also have a lighted tournament board that looks impressive to those playing and watching. Even though each tournament player may not spend a lot on food and beverage, the overall food and beverage sales from players and onlookers is really quite good. Some players will drink alcohol, and almost everyone will order a meal at your place if they are there long enough. The players are able to play pool at our place as long as the tournament is going on, and this encourages them to practice and to join the weekly tournaments.

*Fernie Rivas runs our pool tournaments. He is knowledgeable,*
*and is very popular among players.*

Another thing we have done for the billiard tournaments is institute rules of etiquette. The reason for rules of etiquette is that many players don't always understand when they are sharking an opponent. These rules insure that each player respects the opponent in every situation. Pool does not have the best reputation regarding competitive matches, either in tournaments or playing privately for money. Many times a player will distract another, either purposefully or because they forget their manners. Our rules of etiquette keep everyone aware of the respect they need to show their opponent. The rules also maintain a level playing field for both players in the match, and almost all of our players appreciate playing by these rules.

Here are our nine rules of etiquette:

1. If either player feels that a shot could be a questionable hit, that player is responsible for summoning the referee over to watch the hit. Play must be suspended until the referee arrives. If a referee is not summoned to the pool table to watch the hit, then the call will be in favor of the shooter.

2. If either player moves or picks up the cue ball before both agree that a foul has been committed (or the referee has judged it a foul), that player will forfeit his or her turn at the table, and the incoming player will have the cue ball in hand.

3. If during the final game of a match the observing player unscrews his or her cue or blatantly violates a major rule of etiquette, the shooting player will be awarded that game.

4. Player must not participate in conversation with anyone while opponent is approaching or playing at the table.

5. Player must sit on a stool while opponent is approaching or playing on the table.

6. Each player may take only one five-minute break during the match and only when it's his or her turn at the table.

7. A player will have 15 minutes to arrive at his designated pool table after a match is announced. If late, the match will be forfeited.

8. Players will be given 30 seconds to complete a shot after approaching the tables. (The player will be put on the clock only after obvious excessive delays: violations could result in loss of game.)

9. Final judgments will be made by the tournament director in all instances.

A tournament director with a good attitude is a must for a billiard room that is going to run tournaments. He or she should understand the rules of the game, be fair with all players, and be careful to institute rules of etiquette that ensure players are respectful of their opponents and to the rules of pool. Our current director, Fernie Rivas, embodies all of the traits necessary for a good tournament director. In addition to being a top local player, he understands people and gets along well with customers. There is no question of who is in charge. I give Fernie free reign to make all decisions while running the tournament. This way he gains respect from the players and feels comfortable when he needs to reprimand someone. Not all poolrooms will promote pool tournaments the way we do. You will need to decide if this is something you want for your theme.

Since Danny K's is a large poolroom, we can afford to allow players to stay and play. If I did not have the space or the amount of pool tables we have, I might not be able to offer free pool to players in the tournament. Because we have the extra space players can stick around and play, socialize, and be a part of Danny K's. A very wise person told me years ago, "The most expensive thing in a bar is an empty bar stool." So true.

*Ray McCabe started and has run the Players' League at Danny K's for 23 years.*

# KEEPING THE PLACE CLEAN
# AND NEW

I have greeted people coming into Danny K's who I have not seen for 10 years or so, and they usually say something like, "The place looks great!" The carpet is always clean and upgraded, the bar stools always in good condition, the bar always clean with newer TVs, the pool tables leveled with new cloth. The place in general is maintained with care and with the customers' continued patronage in mind. Many customers spend a good part of their lives at Danny K's, so it is a constant labor of love to keep the place looking nice for them.

Recently we gave the bar a facelift. The stainless steel around the beer taps was beginning to deteriorate as well as the back bar. After 25 years of pouring beer and drinks and serving them, it was beginning to show some wear. So I replaced the stainless steel and made the coverage larger, added lighting for the beer taps and liquor, and repaired and replaced much of the bar back that was beginning to deteriorate. Even though the customers may not say anything, I believe they can feel the change and the difference. These changes and upgrades can alter the overall feel of an establishment.

One advantage a small business has over a corporate entity is that the owner is typically more involved with the everyday process of keeping the place looking nice and upgraded. Change is always a good thing that customers will appreciate, especially if the change enhances features they enjoy, even if they don't quite recognize it at the time.

All of our kitchen help is responsible for cleaning Danny K's. Because we open every day at 11 a.m., someone is at Danny K's cleaning at 7 or 8 in the morning. The place is big with a lot of carpet, so it is vacuumed daily, the tile is mopped, and the bathrooms are completely cleaned. Graffiti is also removed whenever it appears, and in a sports bar, it will appear on occasion. Our policy is: if you see it, remove it. Customers will certainly notice if you don't.

*A football game being shown at Danny K's.*

The owner and manager of a business are like a ham and egg sandwich. The manager (the chicken) has dedicated the egg, but the owner (the pig) is committed. When you become an owner, you will come to understand this riddle. When someone takes a bite of the sandwich, you feel it, usually down to your core.

Customers who have been regulars for years have come to know that we continuously upgrade and are constantly working on making the place nicer. We have developed a reputation for cleanliness and quality, and of course these satisfied patrons tell others.

# BACK OF THE HOUSE OPERATIONS

The back of the house refers to the office—where bookkeeping and daily sales reports take place, money is handled, flyers are made, and so on. Reports can be pulled from the POS system to generate price changes and product changes. Money is counted to balance out the daily sales report, and discounts and comps are reviewed to confirm their validity.

A good fire safe is an important commodity here, because of the possibilities of fire or theft. The safe needs to be heavy and anchored to the floor or wall. Thieves nowadays just pick the safe up and carry it out if it is not heavy and anchored to the floor. Two years ago, Danny K's was broken into, and the safe was picked up and carried out. We thought it was heavy enough. We were wrong. Now we have a metal door going up to the office, a heavy wooden office door, and a 600-pound fire safe that is anchored to the floor. This is a necessary expense. All it takes is one break-in to ruin your month.

The POS system will generate a daily sales report that will give you credit card and cash totals and allow you to close out the previous day and begin anew. It will also prompt you to batch the existing credit cards and show the amount of cash needed to balance out the day. The POS can also give the department totals, so that you know how much draft beer, food, alcohol, etc., has been sold. Of course, you can find other categorical totals in the program of your POS system.

Once the daily sales report has been posted, your bookkeeper can enter the totals into a ledger so you can keep a running bank total. Also, the bookkeeper can enter everything into your bookkeeping program. We use QuickBooks at Danny K's and have since we opened. I find it to be a complete program that categorizes all of our expenses and determines profit and loss. We also write checks to vendors on QuickBooks, and it gives us an accurate balance in our checking account.

Note the comps and discounts for some of the departments below. Comps are drinks that are purchased for customers and free lunches for management and the owner (me). Discounts are the half-price meals we offer to employees. Comps and discounts are figured into the percentages when determining cost of sales. Some restaurants may not figure item costs this way. We do, because it keeps us focused on the total cost of the item. Here is a sample of a Profit & Loss sheet generated by QuickBooks. The numbers are not real, but the categories and departments of profit centers are ones we use.

### Danny K's, Inc.
### Profit & Loss
### January 1 through September 10, 2016

**Ordinary Income/Expense Income**

| | |
|---|---|
| 4000-Food Sales- Taxable | |
| 4001-Food Comp | -4,247.32 |
| 4002-Food Discount | -8,037.06 |
| 4000-Food Sales-Taxable-Other | 376,415.76 |
| Total 4000-Food Sales- Taxable-Other | 364,130.38 |
| 4010-Food Sales-Non Taxable | 11,982.38 |
| 4015-Non Alcoholic Beverages | |
| 4016-Non Alcoholic Comps | -1,850 |
| 4015-Non Alcoholic Beverages | 36.390.39 |
| Total 4015-Non Alcoholic Beverages | 34,539.80 |
| 4020-Beer Sales | |
| 4021-Beer Sales Comp | -270.92 |

| | |
|---|---|
| 4020-Beer Sales | 68,293.69 |
| Total 4020-Beer Sales | 68,022.77 |
| 4025-Liquor Sales | |
| 4026-Liquor Sales Comp | -11,561.58 |
| 4025-Liquor Sales | 362,553.18 |
| Total-4025 Liquor Sales | 350,991.60 |
| 4031-Wine Sales Comp | -2065.49 |
| 4030-Wine Sales | 18,536.06 |
| Total 4030 Wine Sales | 16,470.57 |
| 4040-Draft Beer Sales | |
| 4041-Draft Beer Comp | -2,065.49 |
| 4040- Draft Beer Sales | 604,591,09 |
| Total 4040-Draft Beer Sales | 602,418.53 |
| 4050-Billard Table Rentals | 121,870.10 |
| 4090-Merchandise | 320.62 |
| 4095-Special Events-Cover Charge | 5,418.00 |
| 4955-ATM Fee Income | 947.25 |
| **Total Income** | **1,577,112.21** |

**Cost of Goods Sold**

| | |
|---|---|
| 5000-Food Expense | 146.451.42 |
| 5050-Non Alco. Beverage Expense | 11,122.44 |
| 5051-Bottled Beer Exp. | 10,205.80 |
| 5052-Liquor Expense | 58,184.14 |
| 5053-Beverage Juice Mixes | 2,139.26 |
| 5056-Wine Expense | 5,757.67 |
| 5057-Draft Beer Exp.. | 153,426.30 |
| Total GOGS | 387,287.03 |
| Gross Profit | 1,189,825.18 |
| Expense | |
| Payroll Expense | |
| Advance | 1,050.00 |
| CA Dis. | 55.95 |
| CA SDI | -55.95 |

| | |
|---|---|
| FICA | 39,602.87 |
| FUTA Employees part | 1,314.05 |
| SUI | 5,929.11 |
| Bonus | 0.00 |
| Overtime | 29,051.28 |
| Sick Pay | 16,209.19 |
| Taxable Wages-Other | 465,625.85 |
| Total Taxable Wages | 510,886.32 |
| Tips Allocated | -126,788.15 |
| W/H Expense | 3,446.97 |
| Total Payroll Expenses | 435,441.17 |
| 6000-Advertising and Promotion | 9,579.32 |
| 6005-Amortization Expense | 23,552.88 |
| 6010-Auto-Gas | 2,134.66 |
| 6055 Billiard Supplies | 3.890.39 |
| 6056-Billiard Table-Repair/Maintenance | 18,182.95 |
| 6058-Depreciation Expense | 9,574.00 |
| 6060-Credit Card Discount | 21,984.87 |
| 6070-Cash-Over/Short | 2,775.23 |
| 6080-Contributions | 36.38 |
| 6095-Equipment Rental | 4,585.68 |
| 6100-Insurance | 16,835.40 |
| 6193-Kitchen Supplies | 30,536.92 |
| 6200-Accounting & Legal | 22,859.94 |
| 6210-Licenses and Permits | 1,427.35 |
| 6223-Office Supplies | 3,467.36 |
| 6225-Paper/Sanitary Supplies | 1,161.26 |
| 6240-Rent Expense | 97,356.35 |
| 6250-Repairs and Maintenance | 72,345.60 |
| 6260-Security | 1,807.26 |
| 6280-Memberships | 2,859.60 |
| 6320-Telecomm Expense | 45,717.57 |
| 6340-Taxes-Property | 5,782.00 |
| 6341-Taxes for Corporation | 3,464.59 |
| 6350-Telephone Expense | 6,744.80 |

| 6360-Trivia Game Rental | 5,433.67 |
| 6390-Uniforms/Towel Service | 1,370.36 |
| 6400-Utilities | 31,349.64 |
| Total Expenses | 844,945.04 |
| Net Ordinary Income | 344,880.14 |

| Other Income/Expense | |
| Other Expense | |
| 6347-Employee Settlement | 6,800.00 |
| Total Other Expense | 6,800.00 |
| Net Other Income | -6,800.00 |

| **Net Income** | **298,080.14** |

Interpreting the profit & loss statement involves going over each and every category of profit and loss centers that the statement contains. For instance, how do you determine a percentage of gross sales? If you divide the actual cost of sales by the gross in that category, you have your net cost. Here is an example of figuring the cost of draft beer.

To find the monthly cost of draft beer, including domestic and premium, divide the total cost of the beer by the gross sales in the category. $153,426.30 \div 602,418.53 = 25.5\%$. This is the pour cost of draft beer. The lower percentage, the higher profit.

While writing this book I discovered that my pour cost is actually higher than the national average of bars and restaurants. The reason for the discrepancy is that we offer a 25-ounce beer at a discount per ounce. And it's a hefty discount. So after doing some figuring I will need to raise prices on the larger beers. It pays to look at your line items on a regular basis, even after 25 years.

Another reason the profit and loss is so important is that you can see in front of you where most of the monthly outlay is going. If there is a spike in food cost, for instance, you can search further into how much you are paying for food. (There are also programs that allow you to figure a net food cost and keep it at a percentage that you are happy with. I prefer to look at what works with the clientele, though, instead of working off percentages.)

You can see the various expenses involved in operating a business such as Danny K's by the P & L. In the beginning, you will want to keep all business costs at a minimum. If you see a spike in a particular category, then you should immediately discover the reason for that surge in cost. If it is food, you can let the kitchen head know about the rise in food cost. If alcohol is higher than normal, speak with bar managers and bartenders.

Generally, if you are proactive in finding the rise in cost and seeking out the cause, you will resolve the issue just by probing and letting everyone know there is a problem.

For people seeking to open a business for the first time, look at the various categories listed here. It is almost impossible to predict the number of categories of expenses you will have after you have opened. Each and every expense, while necessary, will cut into your net profit. This is why it is important to study the P & L over time on a regular basis and keep expenses at a minimum and net profit up.

Your office will be where the helm of the operation is. Critical decisions are usually made here, and with bookkeeping, POS monitoring, menu alterations, employee scheduling, figuring payroll and daily promotions, it will be the central command post of your business. Back of the house operations are a critical part of a sports bar or billiard room.

# ADVERTISING AND SOCIAL MEDIA

After Danny K's had been open for a few years, I decided to try a few cable TV commercials. I wrote and starred in all three, and they were a moderate to big hit in Orange County. A local TV station, called the Orange County News Network was offering a great deal on shooting a commercial and giving special rates, if you spent enough money with them. So I decided to be a local star for a while. This was when the Budweiser frogs were popular, and sports fans were watching skits that were advertising for whatever the company was selling. So I decided I would give it a shot and try my hand at some pool commercials.

All the commercials I did had buxom blondes in them, who would ultimately make me look like a fool after she had beaten me in pool, or showed me up somehow. Even though we didn't make a ton of money from this advertising, the commercials made us popular throughout Orange County and put us on the map. I still have people coming in 20 years after these commercials were aired saying, "Hey, you're the guy in the commercial!"

Other than a few other small advertising campaigns we didn't do much advertising, especially in the beginning when we had no money. I found that remembering names and welcoming customers into Danny K's was the best type of advertising, because it created regular customers who came into our place even if they moved out of the area. I developed a reputation for remembering names, and even particular facts about a customer if he had mentioned something during a previous visit, for instance a child in college or a wife being sick. I would always ask about their family or loved ones, and showed true interest in customers. I do that as a general rule anyway, and so it wasn't difficult for me to focus on aspects of their lives that were important to them.

Some people in the restaurant and bar industry call good customer service and special treatment of customers "four wall promotion." The obvious reason it is called this is because you don't need to go outside of your business to do this kind of internal advertising. It can create long-term relationships with customers who may eventually become friends. Typically, a person leaving your establishment will tell 15 others about their experience. If it is a bad one, you may lose business, but if their story about your place is good, this will increase your business, causing a ripple effect that creates more regular customers. These customers that become regulars will truly consider your place a part of their lives. Since your place is a good bar with a great atmosphere, you are offering them something that is overall beneficial.

This is one reason that employee meetings are so important for a bar or restaurant. Employees need to be reminded about the importance of customer service and the atmosphere that needs to be created in your establishment. It is easy for them to forget the vibe that needs to be created and maintained. I found that doing mailers on occasion or passing out flyers did very little as far as introducing new customers to Danny K's. Whenever advertising has worked for us, it was our efforts done on a larger scale and over a period of time. Our commercials were on the air for a couple of years, and made quite an impact. Finally, OCN went out of business and we stopped advertising on TV. I still consider it worth the money spent.

What worked really well in the past few years was using the media giant Yelp to get the word out that we are a sports bar and a desirable alternative to wherever people are going. A sports bar that was within a couple of miles from us closed down a few years ago, so I contacted Yelp and asked what they would charge us for advertising. They charged $1,000 a month to place us in a good position every time someone Yelped "Sports Bar" or "Pool Room." I figured that the sports bar that closed would leave some disappointed customers with no place to go. As it turned out, most of these patrons had never heard of Danny K's, and so this deal with Yelp worked out very well, as many of these patrons decided to give us a try. Most of those people who have visited became regulars.

We have four stars on Yelp, and I make sure that it stays that way. Some sports bars, even national chains, have three stars or less, and this is unacceptable. Yelp is used more than any other referral and rating social media organization in the US, and most people reference Yelp when trying a new restaurant or club. It is of utmost importance to maintain a high rating on all social media. A study on bars and restaurants concluded that 20 percent of customers at a nightclub or bar will typically fall off or not return after a certain period of time. Maybe they move away, or find a bar closer to home so they don't have to drive as far and risk a DUI. For whatever reason, 80 percent will stay regulars, and the 20 percent who quit coming in need to be replenished. This is what good social media marketing can do. Word of mouth with great customer service will aid in this replacement, but it isn't always enough.

I still consider great, personal customer service to be the best kind of advertising. But if you can afford spending some money on social media, that investment should be worth it. The more people are on cell phones, the more social media is important in their lives and in making decisions about where to go and where to spend their money. Social media is definitely the place to advertise for the future.

*We try to help support charities and fundraising events. After 9/11, we hosted a fundraiser that raised money for families of the fallen police and firefighters.*

A web site is also a must in today's digital world. Your web site should highlight daily specials and have professional photos of your place, especially when it is busy. If you have weekly events such as pool tournaments or sporting events being shown, those should be easily found by someone visiting your web site. Your menu in full should be on there as well. Therefore, updating the web site regularly is a necessary function of a successful business today. An outdated web page can turn customers away as they get the impression that your business is also out of date and not worth their time.

Regarding web sites, I would recommend hiring a professional who can show examples of the work she has done for other clients. Because Google will provide a link to your web site when potential customers are doing a broad search, your page will be viewed by many potential clientele who want to see what your place is all about.

The web is now a part of our culture, and cell phones are used as paths to social media, tools for searching the web, even downloading and reading e-books. Because we carry these devices with us every day, make sure that you are taking advantage of the benefits of promoting your business through social media.

# THE POWER OF HABIT

I recently read the book The Power of Habit by Charles Duhigg. It details the importance of creating a good habit for employees to follow, so that job-related tasks will come naturally. I realized after reading this book that I had been creating good habits all along at Danny K's.

We have placed sports pages above the urinals since the first day we opened. We train every new employee to tear out part of the sports page and place it above both urinals. I can go to the restroom on any given day and see the current sports page. I have seen other bars try to do the same thing, and often the newspaper is several days old, which does not have the same effect (quite the opposite!). This is not the employees' fault—it is management who has not trained them in the correct manner.

All of our servers learn the TV system and are capable of changing any TV for customers wanting to watch a specific game. Our employees are taught how to do this when they begin the job, and they understand that it is a required part of their job description to change the TV channel when a customer requests it. And so it becomes a habit. We are one of a few sports bars that change the television when requested, and our employees do not tell our customers to wait while we do something else first.

Cleanliness is also a matter of habit. Our cleaning person comes in at 8 a.m., on most mornings, and goes through the same routine of vacuuming our large area of carpet, cleaning the restrooms, and mopping the slate floors. Also, the pool tables are vacuumed or cleaned with a damp towel every day. When someone comes into Danny K's for the first time, they usually say, "It is nice, big, and clean." This is thanks to the power of habit.

Server attitudes toward customers becomes a habit as well. Again, smiling with a positive attitude is a must, not an option. And after a few shifts, it becomes natural for the waitress or bartender. Customers will expect this behavior from our staff, and we want them to expect it and appreciate it. In fact, it's okay with me if they take it for granted—because they only need to try another establishment to be reminded of the value we provide. By the number of regulars we have made over the past 24 years, it is evident that customers do appreciate consistently friendly service.

Encouraging the habits you want to see repeated makes it easy for employees to adapt to a pattern that is beneficial to your business. They act in a manner that is born out of appreciation instead of obligation. Learning and establishing good habits is pays off in the long run for a small business.

# EMPLOYEE MANUAL

Having a complete employee manual that every employee reads and signs is mandatory in this day and age of litigation and lawsuits. A thorough manual will give the employee a guide of "dos and don'ts" so that if there is any infraction, the manager can refer to the manual that was signed and show them where they violated the rules. Also, the signed employee manual is useful should any future possible actions be taken against the employer by current or former employees or state or federal officials. California, for instance, has become a hotbed for lawsuits regarding unenforced lunch breaks. Therefore, these days it is especially important to spell out in the employee manual the breaks that an employee is allowed and how they will be implemented.

Issues of sexual harassment and employee discrimination also need to be written clearly in the manual. In the case of discrimination or harassment of any kind, the employees need to understand that the operator has an open door policy that invites them to talk with management at any time to discuss something they feel is wrong. These issues need to be addressed immediately, and those in violation need to be reprimanded.

It is always a good idea to hire an attorney who understands state law to help draft a comprehensive employee manual. The attorney will be able to keep your company in compliance with the law and prevent possible future litigation due to actions of management or employees. I contacted the California State Restaurant Association for a recommendation and used the services of a very good business attorney.

Safety procedures and policies and best practices in the kitchen, behind the bar, and on the floor should also be explained in the employee manual. For instance, we do not allow the kitchen staff to clean floor mats before the kitchen is closed for business. If they are cooking something without a floor mat, it may become easy to slip and fall. The employee manual discusses these dangers and general kitchen safety, as well as the protocol to follow if an accident occurs. If management goes into the kitchen and notices that the mats have been cleaned early, it is likely that the employees would be written up for not following company policy.

In a state such as California where Danny K's exists, more attention to detail needs to be paid to the development of a comprehensive employee manual. In the past few years the state legislature has come up with rules that benefit the employee while making such rules difficult for the employer to institute. For instance, mandatory sick pay now guarantees that the employee will have a certain amount of time off per year due to being sick. Because this is now state law, it needs to be placed into the employee handbook, along with all other rights and obligations that are due the employee.

Some items I cover in my own employee manual are as follows:

1. Probationary Period
2. Work Schedules
3. Meal and Rest Break Policy
4. Timekeeping Requirements
5. Pay Days
6. Overtime
7. Vacation

8. Sick Time

9. Holidays

10. Time off to Vote

11. Jury Duty

12. Bereavement Leave

13. Victim of Domestic Violence Leave

14. Military Leave

15. Personal Leave

16. Workers' Compensation Insurance

17. Drug and Alcohol Policy

In California there is a plethora of items to address and place in the employee manual to cover bases for yourself and the employee. What I have listed here is not all, but a cross-section of what needs to be covered in accordance with California employment law. If you Google your own state employee rights and requirements, you can better understand what needs to be in your employee manual. And again, hire an attorney to help draft or at least vet your manual.

Once the employee has read and fully understands the employee manual, she needs to sign a document indicating that she has done so. This will protect your business as well as the employee. After it is signed, indicating that the employee fully understands what was read, then it becomes like a contract, and both employee and employer are protected.

# DEALING WITH LAWSUITS
# AND LITIGATION

Each state has its own laws and restrictions that the operator will need to follow and adhere to. In California, it is important to note that unemployment can only be accepted by an employee if he has not been written up for offenses three or more times. If the employee has only been written up twice, then he will likely receive the unemployment. And so it behooves every operator to make sure that employees are written up for even small infractions that may not seem severe, but creates a paper trail so that if the employee attempts any type of lawsuit or files for unemployment, the employer is covered by documentation.

In California, the laws governing small businesses change every year, and it is incumbent on each business owner to stay abreast of the most recent changes. Because the laws enacted by the state legislature are not generally business friendly, following the letter of the law in regards to state law is necessary.

Here is an example of how Danny K's got into trouble for not researching the current state law. We have never drawn a huge female pool-shooting clientele. So we offered free pool on Tuesday evenings for women. This added a few women players on a typically slow night and contributed some extra business. I knew there may be a problem with offering something to one gender and not the other, but I figured we could drop the offer of free pool if someone objected.

It wasn't that simple. The state legislature had passed a law that if a business discriminated against a gender, the person or persons suffering the discriminatory act are entitled to a certain amount of money. And they could sue on behalf of all persons who had been violated. Of course, a couple of law students from San Diego went around searching for advertised Ladies Nights at any business and sued each and every owner of these businesses offering something free for women. What did the businesses do? Settle out of court to prevent a class action lawsuit from occurring. It cost us a lot of money because we had not fully understand the letter of the law.

From this point on, I learned to play by the rules of the State of California. And then I was sued by an employee who claimed he was not receiving all his lunch breaks. Since I may not be legally able to speak on this subject due to a settlement clause, let's just say that "whatever the state wants, the state can have." And now all my employees take a mandatory break every few hours, even though to a person they would prefer to keep working and forego the break.

As a business owner, I can see that some laws are not realistic for small businesses and many are flat unreasonable. Even when a law may seem idiotic, obey the law and then let it go without resenting those who made the law.

As I stated in the previous chapter on employee manuals, I contacted the California Restaurant Association and was referred to an attorney who understands California law. He helped us modify our employment manual and has given me terrific advice regarding employees and compliance with state law. I would recommend you have an attorney or someone who knows state laws inside and out on your team who you can contact immediately if you fear you may be in violation of any state or federal law. Even if you are not in violation, the expert can help you stay within the boundaries of the law.

We were sued a few years ago by an employee who claimed that she was terminated because she was pregnant, instead of because of her habitually bad attitude. This was almost comical, because I was able to prove that I had three other employees who had been pregnant at one time during their employment here. All had their children and continued working at Danny K's after giving birth.

Where I made a mistake in this particular situation is that I didn't write the woman up when she was particularly negative with customers. Remember how important documentation is in this business. I always say, "When in doubt, write the person up." If I see an employee who is not abiding by the employee manual, I no longer hesitate to write it up. It protects the business.

Another lawsuit we had to deal with was an incident with an intoxicated customer who was standing outside in the front of Danny K's, having what appeared to be a friendly conversation with one of his friends. This was later in the evening, around midnight or so. I had seen them talking earlier, and I had come inside and was at the front desk, when I heard a loud "bam!" I noticed the blinds covering the window on the left side of the entryway moved back and forth, and thought at first that it was a gunshot. I ran outside immediately to investigate. The intoxicated man had taken a swing at his friend and missed, putting his fist and arm through the window. So when I walked outside and saw the lacerated arm hanging by his side, I immediately dialed 911 for the paramedics to attend to him. His arm was hemorrhaging blood, and he was stunned and staring at his wounded appendage.

When he was taken to the hospital, not only did he have a lot of alcohol in his bloodstream, he also had a substantial amount of amphetamines, which is probably why he decided to take a swing at his friend in the first place.

We waited for some kind of lawsuit, and it finally came. He sued us for a million dollars based on the fact that the plate glass window at Danny K's was not tempered glass, and did not shatter upon impact. When we had opened in 1994, the City of Orange had not required that we replace the existing glass with tempered glass.

The man used a law firm in Los Angeles that was in the habit of suing business owners, and my liability insurance company immediately put an attorney on the case. He spoke with me on numerous occasions, and we had a good strategy with which to proceed. The law firm representing this man thought they had a good case, and every time we won at a lower level, they appealed to a higher court. Eventually, the Supreme Court of California decided that they had no case, and denied even hearing it.

This is not the only instance we experienced that proved settling out of court is not always the answer. We once had a case where a customer slugged someone, again in the front of Danny K's. This time we had it on tape, and luckily too, because the plaintiff wanted to make us liable for not having enough security. The cameras proved this was false. We won this case as well.

Still, California is one of the most litigious states in the nation, and it behooves all business owners to follow the letter of the law. Of course, some lawsuits will happen no matter what kind of precautions you take. It is important to take these lawsuits in stride, no matter how unfair they may appear. Remember, losing your temper is never good for business.

We train all employees the right way to handle customers who are difficult and who may present some form of problem to other customers or to Danny K's employees. For instance, our security guards are called "Door Hosts" and are social with the clientele. I call this "Active Security," which means that the door hosts introduce themselves to customers and welcome them to Danny K's.

I have been to nightclubs before where numerous bouncers are edgy, waiting for a fight or melee to break out. Customers noticing this stance may become anxious themselves, and it may actually encourage some sort of violence. By being gregarious with the clientele and letting them know that you are a friend, they will alert the security if something does happen. This active way of dealing with customers is better for employees as well. It creates less stress and connects them with the clientele in a positive way.

To relieve the stress and possibilities of a lawsuit, read up on your own particular state's regulations and recent lawsuit activity. This will create parameters for what you can and cannot do in the process of running and promoting your business. I always err on the side of caution.

# SEPARATING BUSINESS FROM YOUR PRIVATE LIFE

I was on a vacation with my wife and daughter 12 years ago, and noticed that my mind was still focused on Danny K's. I wasn't allowing myself to enjoy the trip and give the attention to my wife and daughter that they needed. I looked at myself in the mirror of the hotel we were in and told myself, "This is ending right now. I will no longer be distracted by my business. I owe it to my wife and daughter to focus on them when I am not at work."

I was able to let the business go at that moment, and I was able to carry it over when we arrived home from vacation. With that commitment in mind, I was soon able to not think or worry about business when I was home. If a business owner cannot achieve this ability to separate from running the operation, it will have a negative effect on personal relationships, mental and physical health, and even on the success of the business.

I don't need to elaborate on the effects stress has on the state of physical health of entrepreneurs. There are mountains of studies indicating negative consequences from taking stress home and never releasing it. Problems include high blood pressure, stroke, heart attack, and countless diseases related to worrying during all waking hours about business. The immune system can also become compromised and allow diseases to invade the body when we are under tremendous amounts of stress. Releasing the worries of business will help bring about physical well-being and better mental health.

Another benefit of releasing the stress of work is the effect it can have on employees. I have told my managers and employees not to worry about their job when they are not here. When they are at work, I want the very best from them. And I get the best from them. They are happier in their private lives, and they are fresh when they come to work, because business is left at the door while they are away. They are overall happier human beings, and it shows in their work.

This also has a good effect on customers. They can see that servers give their full attention and are happy workers, which allows them to be happy as well. So the overall effect on your business is positive.

I recently sat at my bar next to a young man in his late 20s who found out I was writing this book, and asked me what I thought was the most important thing about running a small business. He was working for a pest control company and wanted to branch out on his own and start his own company. I thought about his question for a couple of minutes, and told him what I thought were the most critical aspects of running a small business.

Separating business from private life was at the top of the list. And I explained that to become a good businessman requires becoming a well-rounded human being. Working 10 hour days, focusing special talents and ambition in a particular business field, requires energy and a large part of the human soul. To do this right, the person needs to be well-rested and fresh each and every day he or she goes to work.

I also explained that family in his life should be a higher priority than his business. So that when at work business is the major focus and at home, family is paramount. It is a way of having presence of mind in both situations. He had been focused on business

24/7, and even when he was home he was obsessively thinking about the company.

I recommended to him that he let the owner of his company know that he needed to spend more time with family, because he felt he was neglecting his wife and kids. Also, that he would still work a ten-hour day, but after, say 6 p.m., he would take no phone calls and do no business. He had been working via phone and computer almost around the clock.

We also talked about his wife and kids, and how they needed him at this time in their lives. And how much he was missing out by not creating great memories with his family. He could really see that he was way too caught up in his business.

He paid careful attention to what I said and told me that he would implement my suggestions right away. I also noticed that his demeanor changed as I was speaking with him. His voice was not as loud as before and he seemed to calm down some.

The irony of this story is that he will become a better business-man because of this, even though spending less time on business. One reason for this is that he will become happier in both parts of his life. He also gets the benefits of a more whole and happy family life. His marriage will probably improve as well. Sometimes spouses don't say much until it is too late, and they are fed up with playing second fiddle.

*My daughter Kelsey and me in 1997 when she was about a year old. Even though I had a very demanding job, I made sure I spent a lot of time with her.*

I believe I helped him, just by suggesting what I have practiced for the past 15 years. He was very appreciative and I hope will act on this right away. I think he just needed a nudge in that direction.

Life is too short to not set up boundaries so we can experience and enjoy the important aspects of our lives.

This is difficult for many business owners to understand, that good mental health translates into happier employees and better business practices and outcomes overall. That the ambience of your establishment will be nicer and more welcoming. Most corporations do not follow this model, which is unfortunate for their employees. If employees are required to bring home the stress of work, they will not perform as well on the job. Harmony among employees makes for a healthier, happier atmosphere for the establishment.

In the beginning, when opening my business, I lived and breathed all the activities and all that went on at Danny K's. I understand how someone just opening a business can become engulfed in it. It needs this attention in the beginning. Like a crying baby, someone needs to be around 24/7 who feels deeply for the child.

Making sure customers are greeted correctly, that the food is coming out of the kitchen in the right way, that employees are busy and not standing around. I was there seven days a week in the beginning. I think this can be necessary at this stage. At some point, though, after the child has begun to walk and can exist somewhat on its own or with the supervision of someone else, it's important to be able to let it go, and not think about it when you are not there.

It is a leap of faith, not worrying about the business, but overall separating work life from personal life is a healthy way to handle your business once it is up and running the way you want it. I was able to put day bartenders in charge and train them to take over. This also instilled in them the need for good customer service and in overseeing employees in a responsible way.

If you can learn the essentials of what makes your business tick, then at some point you can train others to take over for you. After a few years this should be a goal for all owners. Then we can truly enjoy the fruits of our labor.

# THE DESIDERATA

I am adding this chapter because in a business such as this one, which is large and full of many complexities and potential difficulties, it's important to keep everything in perspective.

When I opened Danny K's 25 years ago and was in fear of going under and losing everything I had, I was able to retain a positive attitude. This is due to my philosophy of life: that no matter what happens, life will go on and God still has a plan for us, individually. I am not very religious, but I do believe in God and think that He has a hand in each of our destinies.

I am not saying that it is necessary to believe in God to make your business a success, or even to have a positive outlook. I am saying that a belief in a higher power will make things easier when times get rough. If we believe that this higher power has some control over our destiny, then it's easier to find the positive when things go awry.

Max Ehrmann wrote the "Desiderata," a prose poem, in 1927. I believe it has some great insights on weathering the storms of life. And in this business, believe me, a storm will come. I have a large copy of the "Desiderata" hanging over my desk at Danny K's. When I am working, making menu changes, or doing the daily sales report, I'll sometimes look up and read a few lines. It reminds me to always stay calm and not take life too seriously. It gives me perspective.

# THE DESIDERATA

Go placidly amid the noise and the haste, and remember what peace there may be in silence. As far as possible, without surrender, be on good terms with all persons.

Speak your truth quietly and clearly, and listen to others, even to the dull and ignorant, they too have their story.

Avoid loud and aggressive persons; they are vexations to the spirit. If you compare yourself with others, you may become vain or bitter, for always there will be greater and lesser persons than yourself.

Enjoy your achievements as well as your plans. Keep interested in your own career, however humble, it is a real possession in the changing fortunes of time.

Exercise caution in your business affairs, for the world is full of trickery. But let this not blind you to what virtue there is; many persons strive for high ideals, and everywhere life is full of heroism.

Be yourself. Especially do not feign affection. Neither be cynical about love, for in the face of all aridity and disenchantment it is as perennial as the grass.

Take kindly the counsel of the years, gracefully

surrendering the things of youth.

Nurture strength of spirit to shield you in sudden misfortune. But do not distress yourself with dark imaginings. Many fears are born of fatigue and loneliness.

Beyond a wholesome discipline, be gentle with yourself. You are a child of the universe no less than the trees and the stars; you have a right to be here.

And whether or not it is clear to you, no doubt the universe is unfolding as it should. Therefore, be at peace with God, whatever you conceive Him to be. And whatever your labors and aspirations in \the noisy confusion of life, keep peace in your soul. With all its sham, drudgery and broken dreams, it is still a beautiful world. Be cheerful. Strive to be happy.

When I began seeing Pierce Ommaney, my mentor, in 1969, I noticed that he had a copy of the "Desiderata" hanging on the wall near the front door. We discussed it many times in therapy, and he considered it a poem that had a special meaning and guidance for all who were taking a look at themselves and trying to become happier in their lives.

# MY METAMORPHOSIS

When I opened the doors to Danny K's Cafe and Billiards in January of 1994, I was very introverted and reserved, and would watch people from afar. I was 43 years old, had never married, and had only had a few girlfriends over the years. I was definitely not prepared to become the social butterfly that I needed to become after opening my business. To say this was a difficult transition is a real understatement.

Introducing myself to customers who were coming into my place and experiencing what I had to offer was a scary proposition for me. Customers were typically nice to me, but I sincerely did not know what to say. I had always been introverted, and would stand by myself in a bar or party, chalking it up to just being shy. I knew that I needed to meet people and socialize because this was part of the internal marketing I needed to do for Danny K's.

It took courage for me to walk up to a table of customers, introduce myself, and ask how they were doing. And in the lull of conversation think of something to say. My heart rate would always go up, and I would feel the fear of the unknown. What might happen at that table if I stumbled over words or could not think of something to say? Of course, everyone was always glad to meet the owner, and I developed a real ability for remembering people and their names. Albeit my fears were unjustified, if I had not opened this business, I would still be the shy, reserved person who stood in the corner and observed from afar. (Some people probably wish I was still that person!)

As the owner of Danny K's, I would meet people at the bar and introduce myself, and to this day I will do the very exact thing in most social situations. I enjoy sitting at a bar because I can meet all these interesting people. Some people are born with this social quality; I had to learn and acquire it.

I have discussed previously the power of habit, of doing something over and over so that it becomes a routine. Meeting new people became routine for me and now is very natural. Of course, this applies to my private life now as well. I have been president of a local Rotary Club twice, and have spoken on how to open and operate a place like Danny K's on several occasions. Actions can become natural if practiced.

*On occasion we will have a band for an anniversary party. Me on the pedal steel.*

I have also learned to play pedal steel guitar since my father passed away in 1977. It was special that he willed it to me. I took a few lessons, and then in 2002 I was in charge of getting the band together for my Rotary Club. I needed to learn the instrument better, and so I played numerous gigs with a musician who would let me sit in and play with him. This took courage on my part, because the pedal steel is used many times as a lead instrument. I eventually got good enough to play a set with Brie Harlowe at the Coach House in San Juan Capistrano. I played three times there, and the first time I had stage fright so bad I was sweating profusely. The second time I felt more comfortable and did pretty well. The third time was a charm, and I nailed it. This was all due to the fact that I had the courage to go out on a limb and leave my comfort zone.

I've learned so much from this business and have grown into a better human being. I used to judge people for smoking cigarettes. But seeing my smoking customers spend money in my place helped me understand that they didn't deserve judgment; they just had a problem with addiction. We all have our personal issues, and as unpleasant as smoking was, I learned to allow them that habit.

I have also learned to give people the benefit of the doubt, and wait before I judge something that they do. Things are not always what they appear to be on the surface, and so I allow events to play out so I can see what is really happening. Usually, the truth will emerge, and it is usually somewhat different from what we initially judged it to be. If I jump to a conclusion based on something I've observed and then overreact, I will always go up to the person and apologize. Humility is an incredibly important virtue to learn when owning a business—it's not something you can get by without.

We are all works in progress. Getting to know many of my customers helped me see the good qualities in others that I didn't yet possess. Maybe they were more forgiving, or more courageous. This understanding led me to appreciate people more and allowed me to glean some wisdom from each of them.

I hope that reading about my experiences in opening this business will give you a leg up in opening a sports bar, poolroom, or tavern. This has been my life for 25 years, and I have appreciated every bit of it. Through all my experiences, the total losses and failures, the brimming victories, the sacrifices needed to push the business forward, I now know this: If this is your true dream, you can succeed.

Sometimes I have had to go against my own grain to accomplish things at Danny K's. I have had to learn—the hard way—many of life's lessons about humility, sacrifice, and hard work. Often, learning lessons is unpleasant; however, each lesson is a rare and special gift, and now I'm grateful for even the challenging times because they taught me something. I hope this book has taught you something too, so we can both benefit from my hard-won knowledge.

I have had to venture further than I ever knew I was capable of in order to succeed. And I go willingly and with courage.

I offer you my sincerest best wishes in commencing what may be the greatest endeavor of your life.

# ACKNOWLEDGMENTS

I want to thank my daughter, Kelsey, for help and editing most of this book. When she read the first draft she said, "Dad, it reads well and is interesting, but seems formal to me. Speak with your own voice." This advice allowed me to begin telling more stories, and opened the book up to so many deep wells of past experience and knowledge that I began writing with a flourish. Thank you, Kelsey.

Also, Brian Fairley, for always having faith that I could succeed in my venture, and for loaning me his original business proposal that he used while opening Brian's Beer and Billiards. Brian has always been one of my biggest supporters.

To Pierce Ommanney—rest in peace, my mentor and friend. As I state in the book, without Pierce's psychological help I would not be here. He taught me a different way to live, and that the only thing keeping me from succeeding was me and my internal negativity.

To my mother, Vivian, who always encouraged me and at one time loaned me money to keep Danny K's afloat. She was savvy about business and knew we would make it, but we just needed to believe in it, and dial back our spending.

To Ron Foss, my best friend and pool partner in the '70s and '80s, I could always confide in Ron my deepest problems and secrets. In this life, we need a best friend. Ron has been that to me.

To my original business partner, Richard Johnson, who hired me to sell pool tables in 1980 and became my partner at Danny K's in 1993. Richard had a good business mind and was a capable, solid business partner. And he had faith that this concept could make it.

To my GM, Jami Jun, who started working for Danny K's just after we opened in 1994, and moved up the ladder from front desk attendant, to bartender, manager, and then general manager. Great job, my friend. Thank you for your hard work and dedication to Danny K's.

To my employees at Danny K's, many of whom have worked years for me. Joyce, Eddie, Suzanne, Holly, Lana, Marco, Frank, Maria, Lupita, and countless others who have helped my business stay profitable, and come in day in and day out with the gift of a positive attitude.

And, the most important acknowledgment, to my customers, many of whom have patronized Danny K's for the 25 years we have been open. Without you, we would not exist. Thank you!

I recently came across my original business proposal that I used in opening Danny K's. Here are some pages, faded and all.

Proposal For

Danny K's Cafe & Billiards

In the past years of owning and operating related businesses we have been searching for a billiard room location. Based on years of research and the popularity of billiards among classes and both genders in the past five years, we believe this business will yield a substantial return for its owners, Richard Johnson and Danny Kuykendall.

The location of this particular facility, the available parking, and the low monthly rent make this a very unique situation, not to be found in any part of Orange County.

This proposal outlines the projections and estimates of this opportunity.

## LOCATION AND FACILITY

Danny K'S will be located in an industrial area at 1096 North Main street in Orange California. Main street is a well travelled street, and visibility is excellent. This location is only 6 blocks east of the 57 freeway, two miles north of the 22 and 5 freeways and 4 miles south of the 91 freeway. It is centered in a major Southern California entertainment area, with Anaheim Stadium and Disneyland nearby. The Anaheim Sports Arena, under construction at this time, is less than a mile away. The Stadium Drive-In Theatres are wihin a few blocks away.

With government restrictions making billiard rooms more and more difficult to open, this location presents an opportunity generally not found in Orange County.

## THEME AND ATMOSPHERE

The successful development of a theme and
creation of atmosphere will take place through utilization
of these assets:
1) Knowledge, through experience, in creating an
atmosphere conducive to good business.
2) Danny Kuykendall's reputation in the billiard
community as a professional ethical player.
3) Taking advantage of this facility's unusual physical
assets, (i.e., size, location).

Danny K.'S will be one of the finest billiard
establishments in Southern California. Special attention
will be paid to the condition of the pool tables and the
needs of our players. A warm, cozy atmosphere will be
created by the orderly layout of the tables; uplifting,
however not overly abrasive music through a good sound
system, and quick, attentive service from our employees.
We will also encourage the playing of darts and sports
viewing via wide screen TV's and satellite projection.
We will also be serving a varied, thorough menu of
prepared dishes from our kitchen. These and other measures
will result in obtaining the following element missing in so
many recreational facilities today, FUN!

PROMOTIONS

Promotion of Danny K.s will consist of the following:

1. Word of mouth spread throughout Orange County through contacts made by Danny Kuykendall and Golden West Billiard Supply.

2. Flyers distributed in the immediate commercial and industrial areas to stimulate the daytime lunch crowd.

3. Continuos in-house promotion of pool tournaments that encourage customer's participation on the slower nights of the week. Also, the encouragement of women's events.

4. Personal visitations to the immediate surrounding businesses to encourage and stimulate intra-company pool tournaments.

Our realization and dedication to the promotion of tournaments and new, exciting events is an essential ingredient to the success of Danny K.'s.

MANAGEMENT OPERATIONS AND GUIDELINES

The owners of Danny K.'s understand the importance
of competent organization and enthusiastic management.
All employees and management will be screened for criminal
and work history, and attitude in dealing with the public.
All employees will attend an Alchohol Beverage Control LEAD
seminar, that teaches proper service guidelines such as;
recognizing proper I.D.s; when to not serve alchoholic
beverages to a customer; serving free non-alchoholic
beverages to designated drivers; etc. A security gaurd will
be on the premises from dark until closing monitoring the
behavior of the customers, inside the building and in the
parking lot.

Monthly meetings will be held for employees and
management to discuss daily operations, employee-management
problems, and basically to establish an employee-management
line of communication.

Women working as hostesses and waitresses will be
smartly dressed with clothes bearing the theme and logo
of Danny K.'s, however not to attract or arouse the male
customers. Men waiters and hosts will also wear clothes
bearing a theme of Danny K.'s. All employees greeting the
public will realize the importance of quick, attentive
service, and an overall good, happy attitude in dealing with
customers.

## SALES FORECAST

In constructing a sales forecast, we estimated conservatively revenues from pool table time, food, and vending machines. We based all projections on familiarities with billiard rooms in Orange County and deductive reasoning related to this particular location and possible marketing pool.

Most importantly these revenues will be accomplished by dynamic, enthusiastic and competent management. Areas of management that will develop the business are:

1) Development of a theme.

2) Consistent treatment and concern for customers and employees.

3) Effective advertising

4) Cleanliness and customer service

5) Innovative and profitable promotions

## SALES FORECAST (FIRST YEAR)

| TAXABLE SALES 1 | MONTH | ANNUAL |
|---|---|---|
| Beverages 2 | $84,000 | $1,008,000 |
| Food 3 | 30,200 | 362,400 |
| TOTAL: | $114,200 | $1,370,400 |

### OTHER INCOME

| | MONTH | ANNUAL |
|---|---|---|
| Video games & other vending 4 | 2,250 | 27,000 |
| Pool (On Time) 5 | 32,880 | 394,560 |
| Coin-Op Pool 6 | 3,700 | 44,400 |
| TOTAL: | $38,830 | $465,960 |

1) Estimates in line with other pool rooms in Orange County.

2) Based on sales of soft drinks, wine and beer.

3) Based on sales of 150 meals per day (including appetizers and more expensive meals).

4) Based on 2 video games, 2 dart machines and a juke box.

5) Three coin-ops at 30,00 per day per table

PRO-FORMA INCOME STATEMENT, FIRST YEAR

|  | Per Month | % of Sales | Annual |
|---|---|---|---|
| GROSS SALES | $150,780 | 100 | $1,809,360 |
| Less cost of Goods | 27,266 | 18 | 327,192 |
| GROSS PROFIT | $123,514 | 82 | $1,482,168 |
| | | | |
| OPERATING EXPENSES | | | |
| Fixed | $50,600 | 33 | $607,200 |
| Labor | 27,932.50 | 18 | 335,190 |
| Other | 8,725 | 6 | 104,700 |
| TOTAL: | $87,257 | 57 | $1,047,090 |
| | | | |
| NET INCOME BEFORE TAX | $36,256.50 | 16 | $435,078 |